Hol

Canons,
Order of Preparation, and
Prayers After Holy Communion

According to the usage of
Holy Trinity Monastery

HOLY TRINITY PUBLICATIONS
The Printshop of St Job of Pochaev
Holy Trinity Monastery
Jordanville, New York

Printed with the blessing of
His Eminence, Metropolitan Hilarion
First Hierarch of the Russian Orthodox Church
Outside of Russia

Second Edition

The Rule for Holy Communion
© 2017 Holy Trinity Monastery

PRINTSHOP OF
SAINT JOB OF POCHAEV

An imprint of

HOLY TRINITY PUBLICATIONS
Holy Trinity Monastery
Jordanville, New York 13361-0036
www.holytrinitypublications.com

ISBN: 978-0-88465-488-9 (paperback)
ISBN: 978-0-88465-330-1 (Saddlestitch)
ISBN: 978-0-88465-461-2 (ePub)

Library of Congress Control Number 2017948794

Psalms taken from *A Psalter for Prayer*, trans. David James (Jordanville, New York:
Holy Trinity Publications, 2011). Other Scripture passages taken from the New
King James Version. Copyright © 1982 by Thomas Nelson, Inc.
Used by permission.

Contents

PART 1

The Canons for Holy Communion   5

PART 2

The Order of Preparation for Holy Communion   59

PART 3

The Prayers after Holy Communion   91

APPENDIX 1

Sunday Troparia   99

APPENDIX 2

On the Participation of the Faithful
in the Eucharist   103

The Canons for
Holy Communion

According to the usage of Holy Trinity Monastery, the following Canons, Akathist, and Prayers are inserted into the order of Small Compline immediately following the Symbol of Faith. Following the three prayers, we chant "It is Truly Meet..." and Small Compline continues with the Trisagion. If Small Compline is not appointed (e.g., for a Great Feast), this order is preceded by the Usual Beginning and 50th Psalm, and a dismissal immediately follows "It is Truly Meet."

A Supplicatory Canon to our
Lord Jesus Christ

Second Tone

ODE 1

EIRMOS: In the deep of old the infinite Power overwhelmed Pharaoh's whole army, but the incarnate Word annihilated pernicious sin. Exceedingly glorious is the Lord, for gloriously is He glorified.

REFRAIN: *O sweetest Jesus, save us.*

Sweetest Jesus Christ, long-suffering Jesus, heal the

5

wounds of my soul, Jesus, and make sweet my heart, O Greatly-merciful One, I pray Thee, Jesus my Saviour, that being saved by Thee, I may magnify Thee.

O sweetest Jesus, save us.

Sweetest Jesus Christ, open to me the door of repentance, O Jesus, Lover of mankind, and accept me, O Jesus my Saviour, as I fall down before Thee and fervently implore the forgiveness of my sins.

O sweetest Jesus, save us.

O sweetest Jesus Christ, Jesus, snatch me from the hand of deceitful Belial, O Jesus, and make me stand at the right hand of Thy glory, O Jesus my Saviour, delivering me from the lot of those on the left.

O Most Holy Theotokos, save us.

THEOTOKION: O Lady Who gavest birth to Jesus our God, pray for us worthless servants, that by Thy prayers, O Immaculate One, we who are defiled may be delivered from torment, O Spotless One, and enjoy everlasting glory.

Canon to the Most Holy Theotokos

O Most Holy Theotokos, save us.

Distressed by many temptations, I flee to Thee, seeking salvation. O Mother of the Word and Virgin, from ordeals and afflictions deliver me.

O Most Holy Theotokos, save us.

Outbursts of passions trouble me and fill my soul with great despondency. Calm it, O Maiden, by the peace of Thy Son and God, O All-blameless One.

O Most Holy Theotokos, save us.

I implore Thee Who gavest birth to the Saviour and God, O Virgin, to deliver me from perils. For, fleeing now unto Thee for refuge, I lift up both my soul and my reasoning.

O Most Holy Theotokos, save us.

Ailing am I in body and soul, do Thou vouchsafe me the divine visitation and Thy care, O Thou Who alone art the Mother of God, for Thou art good and the Mother of the Good.

Canon to the Guardian Angel

O Lord Jesus Christ my God, have mercy on me.

TO JESUS: Vouchsafe me, Thy servant, O Saviour, worthily to sing a song and to praise the fleshless angel, my guide and guardian.

Holy angel of the Lord, my guardian, pray to God for me.

Alone I lie in folly and idleness, O my guide and guardian; forsake not me who am perishing.

Glory to the Father and to the Son and to the Holy Spirit.

Direct my mind by thy prayer to fulfill the commands of God, that I may obtain of God forgiveness of sins, and teach me to hate all wickedness, I pray thee.

Both now and ever and unto the ages of ages. Amen.

THEOTOKION: With my guardian angel, O Virgin, pray for me, Thy servant, to the Gracious One, and teach me to fulfill the commandments of Thy Son and my Creator.

ODE 3

EIRMOS: By establishing me on the rock of faith, Thou hast enlarged my mouth over mine enemies, and my spirit rejoiceth when I sing: There is none holy as our God, and none righteous beside Thee, O Lord.

O sweetest Jesus, save us.

Hearken, O my Jesus, Lover of mankind, unto Thy servant calling with compunction; and deliver me, O Jesus, from condemnation and torment, O only long-suffering sweetest Jesus, plenteous in mercy.

O sweetest Jesus, save us.

Receive Thy servant, O my Jesus, who falleth down with tears, O my Jesus, and save me as one repentant, O my Jesus, delivering me from Gehenna, O Master, sweetest Jesus, plenteous in mercy.

O sweetest Jesus, save us.

O my Jesus, the time Thou gavest me I have squandered in passions, O my Jesus. Reject me not, O my Jesus, but call me, I pray, O Master, sweetest Jesus, and save me.

O Most Holy Theotokos, save us.

THEOTOKION: O Virgin Who gavest birth to my Jesus,

implore Him to deliver me from Gehenna. Thou alone art the protectress of the afflicted, O Thou Who art full of divine grace. And vouchsafe me the life that ageth not, O All-blameless One.

Canon to the Most Holy Theotokos

O Most Holy Theotokos, save us.

I have chosen Thee to be the protection and intercession of my life, O Virgin, Mother of God. Pilot me to Thy haven, O author of blessings, O support of the faithful, O Thou only All-lauded One.

O Most Holy Theotokos, save us.

I pray Thee, O Virgin, to dispel the tumult of my soul and the storm of my grief; for Thou, O Bride of God, hast given birth to Christ, the Prince of Peace, O Only Immaculate One.

O Most Holy Theotokos, save us.

Since Thou broughtest forth Him Who is the Benefactor and Cause of good, from the wealth of Thy loving-kindness do Thou pour forth on all; for Thou canst do all things, since Thou didst bear Christ, the One Who is mighty in power; for blessed of God art Thou.

O Most Holy Theotokos, save us.

I am tortured by grievous sicknesses and morbid passions: O Virgin, do Thou help me; for I know Thee to be an inexhaustible treasury of unfailing healing, O Thou All-blameless One.

Canon to the Guardian Angel

Holy angel of the Lord, my guardian, pray to God for me.
All my thoughts and my soul I have committed unto thee, O my guardian; do thou deliver me from all attacks of the enemy.

Holy angel of the Lord, my guardian, pray to God for me.
The enemy troubleth and trampleth on me and teacheth me always to do his will, but do thou, O my guide, forsake not me who am perishing.

Glory to the Father and to the Son and to the Holy Spirit.
Grant me to sing a song with thanksgiving and fervor unto my Creator and God and to thee, my good angel guardian; O my deliverer, rescue me from foes that do me evil.

Both now and ever and unto the ages of ages. Amen.
THEOTOKION: Heal, O Immaculate One, the most painful wounds of my soul, and drive away the enemies that ever fight against me.

Lord, have mercy. *Thrice.*

SEDALION: O Jesus my Saviour, Thou didst save the prodigal. Jesus my Saviour, Thou didst accept the harlot. And now have mercy on me, O Jesus plenteous in mercy; have compassion and save me, O Jesus my Benefactor, as Thou hadst compassion on Manasseh, my Jesus, only Lover of mankind.

KONTAKION, FOURTH TONE: Show compassion to me, O holy angel of the Lord, my guardian, and leave not me, a defiled one, but illumine me with the light unapproachable, and make me worthy of the heavenly kingdom.

EKOS: Vouchsafe my soul, humiliated by many temptations, the ineffable glory, O holy intercessor and singer with the choirs of the fleshless hosts of God. Have mercy and guard me and illumine my soul with good thoughts, that I may be enriched by thy glory, O my angel; and subdue the enemies who wish me evil, and make me worthy of the heavenly kingdom.

Glory to the Father and to the Son and to the Holy Spirit.

SEDALION: Out of the love of my soul I cry to thee, O guardian of my soul, mine all-holy angel! Protect and guard me always from the hunting of the evil one, and guide me to the heavenly life, teaching and enlightening and strengthening me.

Both now and ever and unto the ages of ages. Amen.

KONTAKION: O protection of Christians that cannot be put to shame, O mediation unto the Creator unfailing: Disdain not the suppliant voices of sinners; but be Thou quick, O Good One, to help us who in faith cry unto Thee: hasten to intercession, and speed Thou to make supplication, Thou Who dost ever protect, O Theotokos, those who honor Thee.

ODE 4

EIRMOS: From a Virgin didst Thou come, not as an ambassador, nor as an angel, but the very Lord Himself incarnate, and didst save me, the whole man. Wherefore, I cry to Thee: Glory to Thy power, O Lord.

O sweetest Jesus, save us.

Heal, O my Jesus, the wounds of my soul, O my Jesus, I pray, and snatch me from the hand of soul-corrupting Belial, O my compassionate Jesus, and save me.

O sweetest Jesus, save us.

I have sinned, O my sweetest Jesus; O Compassionate One, O my Jesus, save me who flee to Thy protection, O long-suffering Jesus, and vouchsafe me Thy kingdom.

O sweetest Jesus, save us.

No one hath sinned, O my Jesus, as have I, the wretched one, but now I fall down praying: Save me, O my Jesus, and grant me life, O my Jesus.

O Most Holy Theotokos, save us.

THEOTOKION: O All-hymned One, Who gavest birth to the Lord Jesus, implore Him to deliver from torment all who hymn Thee and call Thee truly the Theotokos.

Canon to the Most Holy Theotokos

O Most Holy Theotokos, save us.

The turmoil of my passions and the storm of my sins do Thou bestill, Thou Who gavest birth to the Lord and Pilot, O Thou Bride of God.

O Most Holy Theotokos, save us.

O bestow, out of the abyss of Thy compassion, on me Thy supplicant; for Thou didst give birth to the Kind-hearted One and Saviour of all who hymn Thee.

O Most Holy Theotokos, save us.

While delighting in Thy gifts, O Spotless One, we sing a song of thanksgiving to Thee, knowing Thee to be the Mother of God.

O Most Holy Theotokos, save us.

As I lie on the bed of my pain and infirmity, do Thou help me, as Thou art a lover of goodness, O Theotokos, Who alone art Ever-Virgin.

O Most Holy Theotokos, save us.

Having Thee as our staff and hope and as our salvation's unshaken battlement, from all manner of adversity are we then redeemed, O Thou All-lauded One.

Canon to the Guardian Angel

Holy angel of the Lord, my guardian, pray to God for me.

Pray thou to God, the Lover of mankind, and forsake me

not, O my guardian, but ever keep my life in peace and grant me the invincible salvation.

Holy angel of the Lord, my guardian, pray to God for me.
As the defender and guardian of my life I received thee from God, O angel. I pray thee, O holy one, free me from all danger.

Glory to the Father and to the Son and to the Holy Spirit.
Cleanse my defilement by thy holiness, O my guardian, and may I be drawn from the left side by thy prayers and become a partaker of glory.

Both now and ever and unto the ages of ages.
THEOTOKION: Perplexity confronteth me from the evil surrounding me, O Most Pure One, but deliver me from it speedily, for I flee only to Thee.

ODE 5

EIRMOS: O Thou Who art the Light of those lying in darkness and the salvation of the despairing, O Christ my Saviour, I rise early to pray to Thee, O King of Peace. Enlighten me with Thy radiance, for I know none other God beside Thee.

O sweetest Jesus, save us.
Thou art the light of my mind, O my Jesus; Thou art the salvation of my despairing soul, O Saviour. O my Jesus, do Thou deliver me from torment and Gehenna, as I cry: Save me, the wretched one, O Christ my Jesus.

O sweetest Jesus, save us.

Utterly cast down to shameful passions, O my Jesus, I now cry: Stretch down to me a helping hand, O my Jesus, and pluck me out as I cry: Save me, the wretched one, O Christ my Jesus.

O sweetest Jesus, save us.

Carrying about a mind defiled, I call to Thee, O Jesus: Cleanse me from the dirt of sin, and redeem me who slipped down to the depths of evil through ignorance, and save me, O Saviour my Jesus, I pray.

O Most Holy Theotokos, save us.

THEOTOKION: O maiden Mother of God, Who gavest birth to Jesus, implore Him to save all Orthodox monastics and laity and to deliver from Gehenna those who cry: Beside Thee we know no certain protection.

Canon to the Most Holy Theotokos

O Most Holy Theotokos, save us.

Fill my heart with gladness, O Pure One, by giving me Thine incorruptible joy, O Thou Who didst bear the Cause of gladness.

O Most Holy Theotokos, save us.

Deliver us from dangers, O Pure Theotokos, Who didst give birth to Eternal Redemption and the Peace that doth pass all understanding.

O Most Holy Theotokos, save us.

Dispel the darkness of my sins, O Bride of God, by the radiance of Thy splendor, for Thou didst bear the Light Divine and Pre-eternal.

O Most Holy Theotokos, save us.

Heal, O Pure One, the infirmity of my soul, when Thou hast deemed me worthy of Thy visitation, and grant me health by Thine intercessions.

Canon to the Guardian Angel

Holy angel of the Lord, my guardian, pray to God for me.

As one having boldness toward God, O my holy guardian, do thou entreat Him to deliver me from the evils that afflict me.

Holy angel of the Lord, my guardian, pray to God for me.

O radiant light, illumine my soul with radiance, O my guide and guardian given me by God, O angel.

Glory to the Father and to the Son and to the Holy Spirit.

Keep me vigilant who sleep from the evil burden of sin, O angel of God, and raise me up to glorify Him through thy supplication.

Both now and ever and unto the ages of ages. Amen.

THEOTOKION: O Mary, Lady Theotokos unwedded, O hope of the faithful, subdue the uprisings of the enemy, and gladden those who hymn Thee.

ODE 6

EIRMOS: Whirled about in the abyss of sin, I appeal to the unfathomable abyss of Thy compassion: From corruption raise me up, O God.

O sweetest Jesus, save us.

O my Jesus Christ plenteous in mercy, accept me who confess my sins, O Master, and save me, O Jesus, and snatch me from corruption, O Jesus.

O sweetest Jesus, save us.

O my Jesus, no one else hath been so prodigal as I, the wretched one, O Jesus, Lover of mankind, but do Thou Thyself save me, O Jesus.

O sweetest Jesus, save us.

O my Jesus, with my passions I have surpassed the harlot and the prodigal, Manasseh and the publican, O my Jesus, and the robber and the Ninevites, O Jesus.

O Most Holy Theotokos, save us.

THEOTOKION: O Thou Who didst give birth to my Jesus Christ, O Only Undefiled and Immaculate Virgin, cleanse me now, the defiled one, by the hyssop of Thine intercessions.

Canon to the Most Holy Theotokos

O Most Holy Theotokos, save us.

My nature, held by corruption and death, hath He saved from out of death and corruption; for unto death He

Himself hath submitted. Wherefore, O Virgin, do Thou intercede with Him Who is Thy Lord and Son, to deliver me from enemies' wickedness.

O Most Holy Theotokos, save us.

I know Thee as the protection of my life and most safe fortification, O Virgin; disperse the horde of temptations, and drive away demonic vexation; unceasingly I pray to Thee: From corruption of passions deliver me.

O Most Holy Theotokos, save us.

We have acquired Thee as a wall of refuge and the perfect salvation of our souls and a relief in afflictions, O Maiden, and we ever rejoice in Thy light. O Sovereign Lady, do Thou also now save us from passions and dangers.

O Most Holy Theotokos, save us.

Bedridden, I lie supine with sickness now, and there is no healing for my flesh, but to Thee, O Good One Who gavest birth to God and the Saviour of the world and the Healer of infirmities, I pray: From corruption of illness raise me up.

Canon to the Guardian Angel

Holy angel of the Lord, my guardian, pray to God for me.

Free me from every temptation, and save me from sorrow, I pray thee, O holy angel, given to me as my good guardian by God.

Holy angel of the Lord, my guardian, pray to God for me.
Enlighten my mind, O good one, and illumine me, I
pray thee, O holy angel, and teach me to think always
profitably.

Glory to the Father and to the Son and to the Holy Spirit.
Abolish present disturbance from my heart, and strengthen
me to be vigilant in good, O my guardian, and guide me
miraculously to quietness of life.

Both now and ever and unto the ages of ages. Amen.
THEOTOKION: The Word of God dwelt in Thee, O Theotokos, and showed Thee to men as the heavenly ladder;
for by Thee the Most High descended to us.

*Here we say one of the following akathists or one to the
current feast or saint:*

Akathist to Our Sweetest Lord Jesus Christ

KONTAKION 1

O Champion Leader and Lord, Vanquisher of hades,
I, Thy creature and servant, offer Thee songs of
praise, for Thou hast delivered me from eternal death; but
as Thou hast unutterable loving-kindness, free me from
every danger, as I cry:

Jesus, Son of God, have mercy on me!

EKOS 1

Creator of angels and Lord of hosts, as of old Thou didst open ear and tongue to the deaf and dumb, likewise open now my perplexed mind and tongue to the praise of Thy most holy Name, that I may cry to Thee:

Jesus, Most-wonderful, Angels' Astonishment!

Jesus, Most-powerful, Forefathers' Deliverance!

Jesus, Most-sweet, Patriarchs' Exaltation!

Jesus, Most-glorious, Kings' Stronghold!

Jesus, Most-beloved, Prophets' Fulfillment!

Jesus, Most-marvelous, Martyrs' Strength!

Jesus, Most-peaceful, Monks' Joy!

Jesus, Most-gracious, Presbyters' Sweetness!

Jesus, Most-merciful, Fasters' Abstinence!

Jesus, Most-tender, Saints' Rejoicing!

Jesus, Most-honorable, Virgins' Chastity!

Jesus, Everlasting, Sinners' Salvation!

Jesus, Son of God, have mercy on me!

KONTAKION 2

As when seeing the widow weeping bitterly, O Lord, Thou wast moved with pity and didst raise her son from the dead as he was being carried to burial, likewise have pity on me, O Lover of mankind, and raise my soul, deadened by sins, as I cry: **Alleluia!**

EKOS 2

Seeking to understand the incomprehensible, Philip asked: Lord, show us the Father, and Thou didst answer him: Have I been so long with you and yet hast thou not known that I am in the Father and the Father in Me? Likewise, O Incomprehensible One, with fear I cry to Thee:

Jesus, Eternal God!

Jesus, All-powerful King!

Jesus, Long-suffering Master!

Jesus, All-merciful Saviour!

Jesus, my Gracious Guardian!

Jesus, cleanse my sins!

Jesus, take away mine iniquities!

Jesus, pardon mine unrighteousness!

Jesus, my Hope, forsake me not!

Jesus, my Helper, reject me not!

Jesus, my Creator, forget me not!

Jesus, my Shepherd, destroy me not!

Jesus, Son of God, have mercy on me!

KONTAKION 3

Thou Who didst clothe with power from on high Thine apostles who tarried in Jerusalem, O Jesus, clothe also me, stripped bare of all good works, with the warmth of Thy Holy Spirit, and grant that with love I may sing to Thee: **Alleluia!**

EKOS 3

I n the abundance of Thy mercy, O Jesus, Thou hast called publicans and sinners and infidels. Now disdain me not who am like them, but as precious myrrh accept this song:

Jesus, Invincible Power!

Jesus, Infinite Mercy!

Jesus, Radiant Beauty!

Jesus, Unspeakable Love!

Jesus, Son of the Living God!

Jesus, have mercy on me a sinner!

Jesus, hear me who was conceived in sins!

Jesus, cleanse me who was born in sins!

Jesus, teach me who am worthless!

Jesus, enlighten my darkness!

Jesus, purify me who am unclean!

Jesus, restore me, a prodigal!

Jesus, Son of God, have mercy on me!

KONTAKION 4

H aving an interior storm of doubting thoughts, Peter was sinking. But beholding Thee in the flesh walking on the waters, O Jesus, he confessed Thee to be the true God; and receiving the hand of salvation, he cried: **Alleluia!**

EKOS 4

When the blind man heard Thee, O Lord, passing by on the way, he cried: Jesus, Son of David, have mercy on me! And Thou didst call him and open his eyes. Likewise enlighten the spiritual eyes of my heart with Thy love as I cry to Thee and say:

Jesus, Creator of those on high!

Jesus, Redeemer of those below!

Jesus, Vanquisher of the power of Hades!

Jesus, Adorner of every creature!

Jesus, Comforter of my soul!

Jesus, Enlightener of my mind!

Jesus, Gladness of my heart!

Jesus, Health of my body!

Jesus, my Saviour, save me!

Jesus, my Light, enlighten me!

Jesus, deliver me from all torments!

Jesus, save me despite mine unworthiness!

Jesus, Son of God, have mercy on me!

KONTAKION 5

As of old Thou didst redeem us from the curse of the law by Thy Divine-flowing Blood, O Jesus, like-wise rescue us from the snares in which the serpent hath entangled us through the passions of the flesh, through lustful suggestions and evil despondency, as we cry unto Thee: **Alleluia!**

EKOS 5

Having beheld the Creator in human form and knowing Him to be the Master, the Hebrew children hastened to please Him with branches, crying: Hosanna! But we offer Thee a song, saying:

Jesus, True God!

Jesus, Son of David!

Jesus, Most-glorious King!

Jesus, Blameless Lamb!

Jesus, Most-wonderful Shepherd!

Jesus, Guardian of mine infancy!

Jesus, Nourisher of my youth!

Jesus, Praise of mine old age!

Jesus, my Hope at death!

Jesus, my Life after death!

Jesus, my Comfort at Thy judgment!

Jesus, my Desire, put me not then to shame!

Jesus, Son of God, have mercy on me!

KONTAKION 6

In fulfillment of the words and message of the God-bearing prophets, O Jesus, Thou didst appear on earth, and Thou Who art uncontainable didst dwell with men and didst take on our infirmities; being healed through Thy wounds, we have learned to sing: **Alleluia!**

EKOS 6

The light of Thy truth shone upon the world and demonic delusion was driven away, for the idols have fallen, O our Saviour, unable to endure Thy strength. But we, having received salvation, cry to Thee:

Jesus, the Truth, dispelling falsehood!

Jesus, the Light, above all radiance!

Jesus, the King, surpassing all in strength!

Jesus, God, constant in mercy!

Jesus, Bread of Life, fill me who am hungry!

Jesus, Source of Knowledge, give me to drink who am thirsty!

Jesus, Garment of Gladness, clothe me the corruptible!

Jesus, Shelter of Joy, cover me the unworthy!

Jesus, Giver to those who ask, give me sorrow for my sins!

Jesus, Finder of those who seek, find my soul!

Jesus, Opener to those who knock, open my wretched heart!

Jesus, Redeemer of sinners, blot out my transgressions!

Jesus, Son of God, have mercy on me!

KONTAKION 7

Desiring to reveal the mystery hidden from the ages, Thou wast led as a sheep to the slaughter, O Jesus, and as a lamb before its shearer. But as God Thou didst rise from the dead and didst ascend with glory to heaven, and along with Thyself Thou didst raise us who cry: **Alleluia!**

EKOS 7

The Creator hath shown us a marvelous Creature, Who was incarnate of a Virgin without seed, rose from the tomb without breaking the seal and entered bodily the apostles' room when the doors were shut. Wherefore, marveling at this, we sing:

Jesus, Infinite Word!

Jesus, Inscrutable Word!

Jesus, Incomprehensible Power!

Jesus, Inconceivable Wisdom!

Jesus, Inexpressible Divinity!

Jesus, Boundless Dominion!

Jesus, Invincible Kingdom!

Jesus, Endless Sovereignty!

Jesus, Supreme Strength!

Jesus, Power Eternal!

Jesus, my Creator, have compassion on me!

Jesus, my Saviour, save me!

Jesus, Son of God, have mercy on me!

KONTAKION 8

Seeing God wondrously incarnate, let us shun the vain world and set our minds on things divine; for God came down to earth that He might raise to heaven us who cry to Him: **Alleluia!**

EKOS 8

The Immeasurable One was below all things, yet in no way separated from things above, when He willingly suffered for our sake, and by His death our death didst put to death, and by His resurrection didst grant life to those who sing:

Jesus, Sweetness of the heart!

Jesus, Strength of the body!

Jesus, Radiance of the soul!

Jesus, Swiftness of the mind!

Jesus, Joy of the conscience!

Jesus, Well-known Hope!

Jesus, Memory before the ages!

Jesus, High Praise!

Jesus, my Supremely-exalted Glory!

Jesus, my Desire, reject me not!

Jesus, my Shepherd, seek me!

Jesus, my Saviour, save me!

Jesus, Son of God, have mercy on me!

KONTAKION 9

All the angelic nature of heaven doth glorify unceasingly Thy most holy name, O Jesus, crying: Holy, Holy, Holy! But we sinners on earth with lips of dust cry: **Alleluia!**

EKOS 9

We see most eloquent orators voiceless as fish concerning Thee, O Jesus our Saviour; for they are at a loss to say how Thou art perfect man, yet remainest God immutable; but we, marveling at this mystery, cry faithfully:

Jesus, God before the ages!

Jesus, King of kings!

Jesus, Master of rulers!

Jesus, Judge of the living and the dead!

Jesus, Hope of the hopeless!

Jesus, Comfort of those who mourn!

Jesus, Glory of the poor!

Jesus, condemn me not according to my deeds!

Jesus, cleanse me according to Thy mercy!

Jesus, drive from me despondency!

Jesus, enlighten the thoughts of my heart!

Jesus, grant me remembrance of death!

Jesus, Son of God, have mercy on me!

KONTAKION 10

Desiring to save the world, O Sunrise of the East, Thou didst come to the dark occident of our nature and didst humble Thyself even unto death; wherefore, Thy name is supremely exalted above every name, and from all the tribes of heaven and earth Thou dost hear: **Alleluia!**

EKOS 10

King Eternal, Comforter, true Christ! Cleanse us of every stain, as Thou didst cleanse the ten lepers; and heal us, as Thou didst heal the greedy soul of Zacchaeus the Publican, that we may shout to Thee in compunction, crying aloud:

Jesus, Treasury Incorruptible!

Jesus, Wealth Unfailing!

Jesus, Strong Food!

Jesus, Drink Inexhaustible!

Jesus, Garment of the poor!

Jesus, Protection of widows!

Jesus, Defender of orphans!

Jesus, Help of toilers!

Jesus, Guide of pilgrims!

Jesus, Pilot of voyagers!

Jesus, Calmer of tempests!

Jesus, God, raise me who am fallen!

Jesus, Son of God, have mercy on me!

KONTAKION 11

Tenderest songs I, though unworthy, offer to Thee, and like the woman of Canaan, I cry unto Thee: O Jesus, have mercy on me, for it is not a daughter, but my flesh cruelly possessed with passions and burning with fury. So grant healing to me who cry unto Thee: **Alleluia!**

EKOS 11

Having previously persecuted Thee, the Light-bestowing Lamp of those in the darkness of ignorance, Paul heeded the power of the voice of Divine enlightenment and understood the swiftness of the soul's conversion; thus also do Thou enlighten the dark eye of my soul, as I cry:

Jesus, my Most-mighty King!

Jesus, my Most-powerful God!

Jesus, mine Immortal Lord!

Jesus, my Most-glorious Creator!

Jesus, my Most-good Guide!

Jesus, my Most-compassionate Shepherd!

Jesus, my Most-merciful Master!

Jesus, my Most-gracious Saviour!

Jesus, enlighten my senses darkened by passions!

Jesus, heal my body scabbed with sins!

Jesus, cleanse my mind of vain thoughts!

Jesus, keep my heart from evil desires!
Jesus, Son of God, have mercy on me!

KONTAKION 12

G rant me Thy grace, O Jesus, Absolver of all debts, and receive me who am repenting, as Thou didst receive Peter who denied Thee, and call me who am downcast, as of old Thou didst call Paul who persecuted Thee, and hear me crying to Thee: **Alleluia!**

EKOS 12

P raising Thine incarnation, we all extol Thee, and we believe with Thomas that Thou art Lord and God, sitting with the Father and coming to judge the living and the dead. Vouchsafe me then to stand on Thy right hand, who now cry:

Jesus, King before the ages, have mercy on me.
Jesus, Sweet-scented Flower, make me fragrant!
Jesus, Beloved Warmth, make me fervent!
Jesus, Eternal Temple, shelter me!
Jesus, Garment of Light, adorn me!
Jesus, Pearl of Great Price, irradiate me!
Jesus, Precious Stone, illumine me!
Jesus, Sun of Righteousness, shine on me!
Jesus, Holy Light, make me radiant!
Jesus, from sickness of soul and body deliver me!
Jesus, from the hands of the adversary rescue me!

Jesus, from the unquenchable fire and other eternal torments save me!

Jesus, Son of God, have mercy on me!

KONTAKION 13

O most-sweet and all-compassionate Jesus! Receive now this our small supplication, as Thou didst receive the widow's two mites, and keep Thine inheritance from all enemies, visible and invisible, from foreign invasion, from disease and famine, from all tribulations and mortal wounds, and rescue from the torment to come all who cry to Thee: **Alleluia! Alleluia! Alleluia!**

This kontakion we say thrice. Then:

EKOS 1

C reator of angels and Lord of hosts, as of old Thou didst open ear and tongue to the deaf and dumb, likewise open now my perplexed mind and tongue to the praise of Thy most holy name, that I may cry to Thee:

Jesus, Most-wonderful, Angels' Astonishment!

Jesus, Most-powerful, Forefathers' Deliverance!

Jesus, Most-sweet, Patriarchs' Exaltation!

Jesus, Most-glorious, Kings' Stronghold!

Jesus, Most-beloved, Prophets' Fulfillment!

Jesus, Most-marvelous, Martyrs' Strength!

Jesus, Most-peaceful, Monks' Joy!

Jesus, Most-gracious, Presbyters' Sweetness!

Jesus, Most-merciful, Fasters' Abstinence!

Jesus, Most-tender, Saints' Rejoicing!

Jesus, Most-honorable, Virgins' Chastity!

Jesus, Everlasting, Sinners' Salvation!

Jesus, Son of God, have mercy on me!

KONTAKION 1

O Champion Leader and Lord, Vanquisher of Hades, I, Thy creature and servant, offer Thee songs of praise, for Thou hast delivered me from eternal death; but as Thou hast unutterable loving-kindness, free me from every danger, as I cry:

Jesus, Son of God, have mercy on me!

Resume canons on page XX.

Akathist to Our Most Holy Lady the Theotokos

KONTAKION 1

T o Thee, the Champion Leader, we Thy servants dedicate a feast of victory and of thanksgiving as ones rescued out of sufferings, O Theotokos; but as Thou art one with might which is invincible, from all dangers that can be do Thou deliver us, that we may cry to Thee:

Rejoice, Thou Bride Unwedded!

EKOS 1

An archangel was sent from heaven to say to the Theotokos: Rejoice! And beholding Thee, O Lord, taking bodily form, he was amazed and with his bodiless voice he stood crying to Her such things as these:

Rejoice, Thou through Whom joy will shine forth!

Rejoice, Thou through Whom the curse will cease!

Rejoice, recall of fallen Adam!

Rejoice, redemption of the tears of Eve!

Rejoice, height inaccessible to human thought!

Rejoice, depth indiscernible even for the eyes of angels!

Rejoice, for Thou art the King's throne!

Rejoice, for Thou bearest Him Who beareth all!

Rejoice, star that causest the Sun to appear!

Rejoice, womb of the Divine Incarnation!

Rejoice, Thou through Whom creation is renewed!

Rejoice, Thou through Whom we worship the Creator!

Rejoice, Thou Bride Unwedded!

KONTAKION 2

Seeing Herself to be chaste, the holy one said boldly to Gabriel: The marvel of thy speech is difficult for My soul to accept. How canst thou speak of a birth from a seedless conception? And She cried: **Alleluia.**

EKOS 2

Seeking to know knowledge that cannot be known, the Virgin cried to the ministering one: Tell Me, how can a son be born from a chaste womb? Then he spake to Her in fear, only crying aloud thus:

Rejoice, initiate of God's ineffable will!

Rejoice, assurance of those who pray in silence!

Rejoice, beginning of Christ's miracles!

Rejoice, crown of His dogmas!

Rejoice, heavenly ladder by which God came down!

Rejoice, bridge that conveyest us from earth to heaven!

Rejoice, wonder of angels sounded abroad!

Rejoice, wound of demons bewailed afar!

Rejoice, Thou Who ineffably gavest birth to the Light!

Rejoice, Thou Who didst reveal Thy secret to none!

Rejoice, Thou Who surpassest the knowledge of the wise!

Rejoice, Thou Who givest light to the minds of the faithful!

Rejoice, Thou Bride Unwedded!

KONTAKION 3

The power of the Most High then overshadowed the Virgin for conception and showed Her fruitful womb as a sweet meadow to all who wish to reap salvation, as they sing: **Alleluia!**

EKOS 3

Having received God into Her womb, the Virgin hastened to Elizabeth, whose unborn babe at once recognized Her embrace, rejoiced, and with leaps of joy as songs, cried to the Theotokos:

Rejoice, branch of an Unfading Sprout!

Rejoice, acquisition of Immortal Fruit!

Rejoice, laborer Who laborest for the Lover of mankind!

Rejoice, Thou Who gavest birth to the Planter of our life!

Rejoice, cornland yielding a rich crop of mercies!

Rejoice, table bearing a wealth of forgiveness!

Rejoice, Thou Who makest to bloom the garden of delight!

Rejoice, Thou Who preparest a haven for souls!

Rejoice, acceptable incense of intercession!

Rejoice, propitiation of all the world!

Rejoice, goodwill of God to mortals!

Rejoice, boldness of mortals before God!

Rejoice, Thou Bride Unwedded!

KONTAKION 4

Having within a tempest of doubting thoughts, the chaste Joseph was troubled. For knowing Thee to have no husband, he suspected a secret union, O Blameless One. But having learned that Thy conception was of the Holy Spirit, he said: **Alleluia!**

EKOS 4

While the angels were chanting, the shepherds heard of Christ's coming in the flesh, and having run to the Shepherd, they beheld Him as a blameless Lamb that had been pastured in Mary's womb, and singing to Her they cried:

Rejoice, Mother of the Lamb and the Shepherd!

Rejoice, fold of rational sheep!

Rejoice, torment of invisible enemies!

Rejoice, opening of the gates of paradise!

Rejoice, for the things of heaven rejoice with the earth!

Rejoice, for the things of earth join chorus with the heavens!

Rejoice, never-silent mouth of the apostles!

Rejoice, invincible courage of the passion-bearers!

Rejoice, firm support of faith!

Rejoice, radiant token of grace!

Rejoice, Thou through Whom hades was stripped bare!

Rejoice, Thou through Whom we are clothed with glory!

Rejoice, Thou Bride Unwedded!

KONTAKION 5

H aving sighted the divinely-moving star, the Magi followed its radiance; and holding it as a lamp, by it they sought a powerful King; and having reached the Unreachable One, they rejoiced, shouting to Him: **Alleluia!**

EKOS 5

T he sons of the Chaldees saw in the hands of the Virgin Him Who with His hand made man. And knowing Him to be the Master, even though He had taken the form of a servant, they hastened to serve Him with gifts and to cry to Her Who is blessed:

Rejoice, Mother of the Unsetting Star!

Rejoice, dawn of the mystic day!

Rejoice, Thou Who didst extinguish the furnace of error!

Rejoice, Thou Who didst enlighten the initiates of the Trinity!

Rejoice, Thou Who didst banish from power the inhuman tyrant!

Rejoice, Thou Who didst show us Christ the Lord, the Lover of mankind!

Rejoice, Thou Who redeemest from pagan worship!

Rejoice, Thou Who dost drag us from the works of mire!

Rejoice, Thou Who didst quench the worship of fire!

Rejoice, Thou Who rescuest from the flame of the passions!

Rejoice, guide of the faithful to chastity!

Rejoice, gladness of all generations!

Rejoice, Thou Bride Unwedded!

KONTAKION 6

Having become God-bearing heralds, the Magi returned to Babylon, having fulfilled Thy prophecy; and having preached Thee to all as the Christ, they left Herod as a babbler who knew not how to sing: **Alleluia!**

EKOS 6

By shining in Egypt the light of truth, Thou didst dispel the darkness of falsehood; for its idols fell, O Saviour, unable to endure Thy strength; and those who were delivered from them cried to the Theotokos:

Rejoice, uplifting of men!

Rejoice, downfall of demons!

Rejoice, Thou Who didst trample down the dominion of delusion!

Rejoice, Thou Who didst unmask the fraud of idols!

Rejoice, sea that didst drown the pharaoh of the mind!

Rejoice, rock that dost refresh those thirsting for life!

Rejoice, pillar of fire that guidest those in darkness!

Rejoice, shelter of the world broader than a cloud!

Rejoice, sustenance replacing manna!

Rejoice, minister of holy delight!

Rejoice, land of promise!

Rejoice, Thou from Whom floweth milk and honey!

Rejoice, Thou Bride Unwedded!

KONTAKION 7

When Symeon was about to depart this age of delusion, Thou wast brought as a Babe to him, but Thou wast recognized by him as perfect God also; wherefore, marveling at Thine ineffable wisdom, he cried: **Alleluia!**

EKOS 7

The Creator showed us a new creation when He appeared to us who came from Him. For He sprang from a seedless womb and kept it incorrupt as it was, that seeing the miracle we might sing to Her, crying out:

Rejoice, flower of incorruptibility!

Rejoice, crown of continence!

Rejoice, Thou from Whom shineth the Archetype of the resurrection!

Rejoice, Thou Who revealest the life of the angels!

Rejoice, tree of shining fruit whereby the faithful are nourished!

Rejoice, tree of goodly shade by which many are sheltered!

Rejoice, Thou Who hast carried in Thy womb the Redeemer of captives!

Rejoice, Thou Who gavest birth to the Guide of those astray!

Rejoice, supplication before the Righteous Judge!

Rejoice, forgiveness of many sins!

Rejoice, robe of boldness for the naked!

Rejoice, love that vanquishest all desire!

Rejoice, Thou Bride Unwedded!

KONTAKION 8

Having beheld a strange nativity, let us estrange ourselves from the world and transport our minds to heaven; for the Most High God appeared on earth as a lowly man, because He wished to draw to the heights those who cry to Him: **Alleluia!**

EKOS 8

Wholly present was the Inexpressible Word among those here below, yet in no way absent from those on high; for this was a divine condescension and not a change of place, and His birth was from a God-receiving Virgin Who heard these things:

Rejoice, container of the Uncontainable God!

Rejoice, door of solemn mystery!

Rejoice, report doubtful to unbelievers!

Rejoice, undoubted boast of the faithful!

Rejoice, all-holy chariot of Him Who sitteth upon the Cherubim!

Rejoice, all-glorious temple of Him Who is above the Seraphim!

Rejoice, Thou Who hast united opposites!

Rejoice, Thou Who hast joined virginity and motherhood!

Rejoice, Thou through Whom transgression hath been absolved!

Rejoice, Thou through Whom paradise is opened!

Rejoice, key to the kingdom of Christ!

Rejoice, hope of eternal good things!

Rejoice, Thou Bride Unwedded!

KONTAKION 9

All the angels were amazed at the great act of Thine incarnation; for they saw the Unapproachable God as a man approachable to all, abiding with us and hearing from all: **Alleluia!**

EKOS 9

We see most eloquent orators mute as fish before Thee, O Theotokos, for they are at a loss to tell how Thou remainest a Virgin and couldst bear a child. But we, marveling at this mystery, cry out faithfully:

Rejoice, receptacle of the Wisdom of God!

Rejoice, treasury of His Providence!

Rejoice, Thou Who showest philosophers to be fools!

Rejoice, Thou Who exposest the learned as irrational!

Rejoice, for the clever critics have become foolish!

Rejoice, for the writers of myths have faded away!

Rejoice, Thou Who didst rend the webs of the Athenians!

Rejoice, Thou Who didst fill the nets of the fishermen!

Rejoice, Thou Who drawest us from the depths of ignorance!

Rejoice, Thou Who enlightenest many with knowledge!

Rejoice, ship for those who wish to be saved!

Rejoice, harbor for sailors on the sea of life!

Rejoice, Thou Bride Unwedded!

KONTAKION 10

Desiring to save the world, He Who is the Creator of all came to it according to His Own promise, and

He Who, as God, is the Shepherd, for our sake appeared unto us as a man; for, like calling unto like, as God He heareth: **Alleluia!**

EKOS 10

A bulwark art Thou to virgins and to all who flee unto Thee, O Virgin Theotokos; for the Maker of heaven and earth prepared Thee, O Most Pure One, dwelt in Thy womb, and taught all to call to Thee:

Rejoice, pillar of virginity!

Rejoice, gate of salvation!

Rejoice, leader of mental formation!

Rejoice, bestower of divine good!

Rejoice, for Thou didst renew those conceived in shame!

Rejoice, for Thou gavest understanding to those robbed of their minds!

Rejoice, Thou Who didst foil the corrupter of minds!

Rejoice, Thou Who gavest birth to the Sower of purity!

Rejoice, bridechamber of a seedless marriage!

Rejoice, Thou Who dost wed the faithful to the Lord!

Rejoice, good nourisher of virgins!

Rejoice, adorner of holy souls as for marriage!

Rejoice, Thou Bride Unwedded!

KONTAKION 11

Every hymn is defeated that trieth to encompass the multitude of Thy many compassions; for if we offer to Thee, O Holy King, songs equal in number to the sand, nothing have we done worthy of that which Thou hast given us who shout to Thee: **Alleluia!**

EKOS 11

We behold the holy Virgin, a shining lamp appearing to those in darkness; for, kindling the Immaterial Light, She guideth all to divine knowledge, She illumineth minds with radiance and is honored by our shouting these things:

Rejoice, ray of the noetic Sun!

Rejoice, radiance of the Unsetting Light!

Rejoice, lightning that enlightenest our souls!

Rejoice, thunder that terrifiest our enemies!

Rejoice, for Thou didst cause the Refulgent Light to dawn!

Rejoice, for Thou didst cause the river of many streams to gush forth!

Rejoice, Thou Who paintest the image of the font!

Rejoice, Thou Who blottest out the stain of sin!

Rejoice, laver that washest the conscience clean!

Rejoice, cup that drawest up joy!

Rejoice, aroma of the sweet fragrance of Christ!

Rejoice, life of mystical gladness!
Rejoice, Thou Bride Unwedded!

KONTAKION 12

When the Absolver of all mankind desired to blot out ancient debts, of His Own will He came to dwell among those who had fallen from His grace; and having torn up the handwriting of their sins, He heareth this from all: **Alleluia!**

EKOS 12

While singing to Thine Offspring, we all praise Thee as a living temple, O Theotokos; for the Lord Who holdeth all things in His hand dwelt in Thy womb, and He sanctified and glorified Thee and taught all to cry to Thee:

Rejoice, tabernacle of God the Word!
Rejoice, saint greater than the saints!
Rejoice, ark gilded by the Spirit!
Rejoice, inexhaustible treasury of life!
Rejoice, precious diadem of pious kings!
Rejoice, venerable boast of reverent priests!
Rejoice, unshakable fortress of the Church!
Rejoice, inviolable wall of the kingdom!
Rejoice, Thou through Whom victories are obtained!
Rejoice, Thou through Whom foes fall prostrate!
Rejoice, healing of my flesh!

Rejoice, salvation of my soul!
Rejoice, Thou Bride Unwedded!

KONTAKION 13

O All-praised Mother Who didst bear the Word holier than all the saints, accept now our offering and deliver us from all misfortune and rescue from the torment to come those who cry to Thee: **Alleluia! Alleluia! Alleluia!**

This kontakion we say thrice. Then:

EKOS 1

An archangel was sent from heaven to say to the Theotokos: Rejoice! And beholding Thee, O Lord, taking bodily form, he was amazed and with his bodiless voice he stood crying to Her such things as these:

Rejoice, Thou through Whom joy will shine forth!

Rejoice, Thou through Whom the curse will cease!

Rejoice, recall of fallen Adam!

Rejoice, redemption of the tears of Eve!

Rejoice, height inaccessible to human thought!

Rejoice, depth indiscernible even for the eyes of angels!

Rejoice, for Thou art the King's throne!

Rejoice, for Thou bearest Him Who beareth all!

Rejoice, star that causest the Sun to appear!

Rejoice, womb of the Divine Incarnation!

Rejoice, Thou through Whom creation is renewed!

Rejoice, Thou through Whom we worship the Creator!

Rejoice, Thou Bride Unwedded!

KONTAKION 1

To Thee, the Champion Leader, we Thy servants dedicate a feast of victory and of thanksgiving as ones rescued out of sufferings, O Theotokos; but as Thou art one with might which is invincible, from all dangers that can be do Thou deliver us, that we may cry to Thee:

Rejoice, Thou Bride Unwedded!

Supplicatory Canon to our Lord Jesus Christ (continued)

ODE 7

EIRMOS: When the golden image was worshipped in the plain of Dura, Thy three children despised the godless order. Thrown into the fire, they were bedewed and sang: Blessed art Thou, O God of our fathers.

O sweetest Jesus, save us.

O Christ Jesus, no one on earth hath ever sinned, O my Jesus, as I, the wretched one and prodigal, have sinned. Wherefore, I cry to Thee, my Jesus, have compassion on me as I sing: Blessed art Thou, O God of our fathers.

O sweetest Jesus, save us.

O Christ Jesus, I cry: Nail me down with the fear of Thee, O my Jesus, and pilot me to Thy calm haven now, O my compassionate Jesus, that as one saved I may sing to Thee: Blessed art Thou, O God of our fathers.

O sweetest Jesus, save us.

O Christ Jesus, ten thousand times have I, the passionate one, promised Thee repentance, O my Jesus, but wretch that I am, I deceived Thee. Wherefore, I cry to Thee, my Jesus: Enlighten my soul which remaineth unfeeling; O Christ, the God of our fathers, blessed art Thou.

O Most Holy Theotokos, save us.

THEOTOKION: O Thou Who gavest birth to Jesus awesomely and above nature, O All-blameless One, implore Him, O Maiden, to forgive me all the sins that I have committed against my nature, that as one saved I may cry: Blessed art Thou Who didst give birth to God in the flesh.

Canon to the Most Holy Theotokos

O Most Holy Theotokos, save us.

Having willed to accomplish our salvation, O Saviour, Thou didst dwell in the womb of the Virgin and didst show Her to the world as the mediatress; O God of our fathers, blessed art Thou.

O Most Holy Theotokos, save us.

The Dispenser of mercy, Whom Thou didst bear, O Pure Mother, do Thou implore to deliver from transgressions and defilements of the soul those who with faith cry out: O God of our fathers, blessed art Thou.

O Most Holy Theotokos, save us.

A treasury of salvation and a fountain of incorruption is She Who gave Thee birth; a tower of safety and a door of repentance hast Thou proved Her to those who shout: O God of our fathers, blessed art Thou.

O Most Holy Theotokos, save us.

For weakness of body and sickness of soul, O Theotokos, do Thou vouchsafe healing to those who with love draw near to Thy protection, O Virgin, Who for us gavest birth to Christ the Saviour.

Canon to the Guardian Angel

Holy angel of the Lord, my guardian, pray to God for me.

Be merciful to me and entreat God, O angel of the Lord; for I have thee as a defender for the whole of my life, a guide and guardian given me by God forever.

Holy angel of the Lord, my guardian, pray to God for me.

Leave not my wretched soul, which was given thee blameless by God, to be slain by robbers along the way, O holy angel, but guide it to the way of repentance.

Glory to the Father and to the Son and to the Holy Spirit.
My whole soul is disgraced by the evil thoughts and deeds I have brought upon me, but make haste, O my guide, and grant me healing with good thoughts, that I may be inclined always to the right way.

Both now and ever and unto the ages of ages. Amen.
THEOTOKION: O Wisdom of the Most High Personified, for the sake of the Theotokos, fill with wisdom and divine strength all who faithfully cry: O God of our fathers, blessed art Thou.

ODE 8

EIRMOS: O ye works, praise the Lord God, Who descended into the fiery furnace with the Hebrew children and changed the flame into dew, and supremely exalt Him unto all ages.

O sweetest Jesus, save us.
I implore Thee, O my Jesus: As Thou didst redeem the harlot from many sins, O my Jesus, likewise redeem me, O Christ my Jesus, and cleanse my foul soul, O my Jesus.

O sweetest Jesus, save us.
O Jesus, having yielded to irrational pleasures, I have become irrational, O my Jesus; and wretch that I am, I have truly become like unto the beasts, O my Saviour. Wherefore, O Jesus, deliver me from irrationality.

O sweetest Jesus, save us.

Having fallen, O Jesus, into the hands of soul-corrupting thieves, I have been stripped now of my divinely-woven garment, O my Jesus, and I am lying all bruised with wounds. O my Christ, do Thou pour on me oil and wine.

O Most Holy Theotokos, save us.

THEOTOKION: O Theotokos Mary, Who ineffably didst carry the Christ, my Jesus and God: do Thou ever implore Him to save from perils Thy servants and those who praise Thee, O Virgin Who knewest not wedlock.

Canon to the Most Holy Theotokos

O Most Holy Theotokos, save us.

Disdain not those who need Thy help, O Virgin, and who hymn and supremely exalt Thee unto the ages.

O Most Holy Theotokos, save us.

Thou healest the infirmity of my soul and the pains of my body, O Virgin, that I may glorify Thee, O Pure One, unto the ages of ages.

O Most Holy Theotokos, save us.

Thou pourest forth a wealth of healing on those who with faith hymn Thee, O Virgin, and who supremely exalt Thine ineffable Offspring.

O Most Holy Theotokos, save us.

Thou drivest away the assaults of temptations and the

attacks of the passions, O Virgin; wherefore do we hymn Thee unto all ages.

Canon to the Guardian Angel

Holy angel of the Lord, my guardian, pray to God for me.
O good angel, sent by God, support me, thy servant, in my life and forsake me not unto the ages.

Holy angel of the Lord, my guardian, pray to God for me.
O most-blessed one, I hymn thee, O good angel, guide and guardian of my soul unto the ages.

Glory to the Father and to the Son and to the Holy Spirit.
Be unto me a protection and fortification in the judgment day of all men, in which all deeds, both good and evil, shall be tried by fire.

Both now and ever and unto the ages of ages. Amen.
THEOTOKION: Be unto me, Thy servant, a helper and a calmness, O Ever-Virgin Theotokos, and leave me not bereft of Thy protection.

ODE 9

EIRMOS: God the Word, Who came forth from God and Who by ineffable wisdom came to renew Adam after his grievous fall to corruption through eating and Who ineffably took flesh from the holy Virgin for our sake, Him do we the faithful with one accord magnify with hymns.

O sweetest Jesus, save us.

I have surpassed, O my Jesus, Manasseh and the publican, the harlot and the prodigal, O compassionate Jesus, and the robber, O my Jesus, through all my shameful and unseemly deeds, O Jesus; but do Thou forestall me, O my Jesus, and save me.

O sweetest Jesus, save us.

By my passions, O my Jesus, have I, the wretched one, surpassed all those from Adam who have sinned both before the Law and in the Law, O Jesus, and after the Law and Grace, O my Jesus; but by Thy judgments save me, O my Jesus.

O sweetest Jesus, save us.

May I not be parted from Thine ineffable glory, my Jesus, nor may the portion on the left fall to me, O sweetest Jesus; but set me on the right hand with Thy sheep and give me rest, O Christ my Jesus, since Thou art compassionate.

O Most Holy Theotokos, save us.

THEOTOKION: O Theotokos, Who didst carry Jesus, O only unwedded Virgin Mary Who knewest not wedlock, O Pure One, invoke Him, Thy Son and Creator, to deliver those who hasten to Thee from temptation and perils and the fire that is to come.

Canon to the Theotokos

O Most Holy Theotokos, save us.

Turn not away from the torrent of my tears, O Virgin, Thou Who didst give birth to Christ, Who doth wipe away all tears from every face.

O Most Holy Theotokos, save us.

Fill my heart with joy, O Virgin, Thou Who didst receive the fullness of joy and didst banish the grief of sin.

O Most Holy Theotokos, save us.

Be the haven and protection and a wall unshaken, a refuge and shelter and the gladness, O Virgin, of those who flee unto Thee.

O Most Holy Theotokos, save us.

Illumine with the rays of Thy light, O Virgin, those who piously confess Thee to be the Theotokos, and do Thou banish away all darkness of ignorance.

O Most Holy Theotokos, save us.

THEOTOKION: In a place of affliction and infirmity am I brought low; O Virgin, do Thou heal me, transforming mine illness into healthfulness.

Canon to the Guardian Angel

O Lord Jesus Christ my God, have mercy on me.

Have mercy on me, O my only Saviour, for Thou art merciful and kind-hearted, and make me a member of the choirs of the righteous.

Holy angel of the Lord, my guardian, pray to God for me.
Grant me ever to think and do what is useful, O angel of the
Lord, that I may be blameless and strong in infirmity.

Glory to the Father and to the Son and to the Holy Spirit.
As one having boldness toward the Heavenly King, do
thou, with the rest of the bodiless ones, entreat Him to
have mercy on me, the wretched one.

Both now and ever and unto the ages of ages. Amen.
THEOTOKION: Having great boldness toward Him Who
took flesh of Thee, O Virgin, deliver me from fetters
and grant me absolution and salvation through Thine
intercessions.

Prayer to our Lord Jesus Christ

O Lord and Master, Jesus Christ my God, Who for the
sake of Thine ineffable love for mankind at the end
of the ages wast wrapped in flesh from the Ever-Virgin
Mary, I glorify Thy saving providence and care for me, Thy
servant, O Master. I praise Thee, for through Thee I have
learned to know the Father; I bless Thee through Whom
the Holy Spirit came into the world; I bow to Thy most
pure Mother Who served for the dread mystery of Thine
incarnation; I praise the angelic choir as the servants and
singers of Thy majesty; I bless St. John the Forerunner who
baptized Thee, O Lord; I honor also the prophets who
announced Thee; I glorify Thy holy apostles; I celebrate

the martyrs; I glorify Thy priests; I venerate Thy saints and praise all Thy righteous ones. This such countless and unutterable divine choir I, Thy servant, in prayer offer to Thee, O All-compassionate God, and therefore I ask the forgiveness of my sins, which do Thou grant me for the sake of all Thy saints, but especially for the sake of Thy holy compassion, for blessed art Thou unto the ages. Amen.

Prayer to the Most Holy Theotokos

Accept from us Thy unworthy servants, O all-powerful for good, immaculate, Sovereign Lady, Mother of God, these honorable gifts, which can be offered only to Thee, Who art the one chosen out of all generations, and Who hast become higher than all creation, heavenly and earthly. For through Thee the Lord of Powers was with us, and through Thee we came to know the Son of God, and were granted His holy Body and most pure Blood. Therefore Thou art blessed by all generations, the favorite of God, more radiant than the Cherubim, and more honorable than the Seraphim. And now, O All-hymned, most holy Mother of God, cease not to pray for us, Thy unworthy servants, to be delivered from every snare of the subtle one, and from all besetting sins, and preserve us unharmed from every poisonous temptation of the devil. But preserve us to the end uncondemned by Thy prayers; for saved by Thy help and protection, we send up glory, praise, thanksgiving and adoration for all, to the One God, in Trinity and Creator of all, now and ever, and to the ages of ages. Amen.

Prayer to the Guardian Angel

O holy angel of Christ, I fall down and pray to thee, my holy guardian, given to me from holy baptism for the protection of my sinful body and soul. By my laziness and bad habits, I have angered thy most pure light, and have driven thee away from me by all my shameful deeds, lies, slanders, envy, condemnation, scorn, disobedience, brotherly hatred, grudges, love of money, adultery, anger, meanness, greed, excess, talkativeness, negative and evil thoughts, proud ways, dissolute madness, having self-will in all the desires of the flesh. O my evil will, which even the dumb animals do not follow! How canst thou look at me or approach me who am like a stinking dog? With what eyes, O angel of Christ, wilt thou look at me so badly snared in evil deeds? How can I ask forgiveness for my bitter, evil and wicked deeds, into which I fall every day and night, and every hour? But I fall down and pray, O my holy guardian: pity me, thy sinful and unworthy servant *(Name)*. Be my helper and protector against my wicked enemy, by thy holy prayers, and make me a partaker of the kingdom of God with all the saints, always, now and ever, and to the ages of ages. Amen.

The Order of Preparation for Holy Communion

This Order of Preparation is according to the Jordanville Prayer Book.

Through the prayers of our holy fathers, O Lord Jesus Christ our God, have mercy on us. Amen.

Glory to Thee, our God, glory to Thee.

O Heavenly King, Comforter, Spirit of Truth, Who art everywhere present and fillest all things, Treasury of good things and Giver of life: Come and dwell in us, and cleanse us of all impurity, and save our souls, O Good One.

Holy God, Holy Mighty, Holy Immortal, have mercy on us. *Thrice.*

Glory to the Father and to the Son and to the Holy Spirit, both now and ever and unto the ages of ages. Amen.

O Most Holy Trinity, have mercy on us. O Lord, blot out our sins. O Master, pardon our iniquities. O Holy One, visit and heal our infirmities for Thy name's sake.

Lord, have mercy. *Thrice.*

Glory to the Father and to the Son and to the Holy Spirit, both now and ever and unto the ages of ages. Amen.

Our Father, Who art in the heavens, hallowed be Thy name. Thy kingdom come, Thy will be done, on earth as it is in heaven. Give us this day our daily bread, and forgive us our debts, as we forgive our debtors; and lead us not into temptation, but deliver us from the evil one.

Lord, have mercy. *Twelve times.*

Glory to the Father and to the Son and to the Holy Spirit, both now and ever and unto the ages of ages. Amen.

O come let us worship God, our King.

O come let us worship and fall down before Christ, our King and God.

O come let us worship and fall down before Christ Himself, our King and God.

Psalm 22

The Lord is my shepherd; therefore can I lack nothing. He maketh me to lie down in a green pasture; He leadeth me beside the still water. He hath converted my soul; He hath set me on the paths of righteousness, for His Name's sake. Yea, though I walk through the valley of the shadow of death, I will fear no evil, for Thou art with me; Thy rod and Thy staff, they have comforted me. Thou hast prepared a table before me against them that trouble me; Thou hast anointed my head with oil, and Thy cup that inebriateth me, how strong it is! And Thy mercy shall follow me all the days of my life, and I will dwell in the house of the Lord unto length of days.

Psalm 23

The earth is the Lord's, and the fullness thereof; the compass of the world, and all that dwell therein. He hath founded it upon the seas, and prepared it upon the floods. Who shall ascend into the hill of the Lord, or who shall stand in His holy place? Even he that hath clean hands, and a pure heart, who doth not take his soul in vain, nor swear falsely to his neighbor. He shall receive a blessing from the Lord, and mercy from God his Saviour. This is the generation of them that seek the Lord, even of them that seek the face of the God of Jacob. Lift up your gates, O ye princes, and be ye lift up, ye everlasting doors, and the King of glory shall come in. Who is this King of glory? It is the Lord strong and mighty, even the Lord mighty in battle. Lift up your gates, O ye princes, and be ye lift up, ye everlasting doors, and the King of glory shall come in. Who is this King of glory? Even the Lord of hosts, He is the King of glory.

Psalm 115

I believed, so I spake; but I was greatly humbled. I said in my confusion, All men are liars. What shall I render unto the Lord, for all that He hath rendered unto me? I will take the cup of salvation, and call upon the Name of the Lord. I will pay my vows unto the Lord in the presence of all His people. Precious in the sight of the Lord is the death of His saints. O Lord, I am Thy servant; I am Thy servant, and the son of Thine handmaid; Thou hast broken my bonds in sunder. I will offer unto Thee a sacrifice of thanksgiving, and will call upon the Name of the Lord. I will pay my vows unto the Lord in the presence of all His people, In the courts of the Lord's house, even in the midst of thee, O Jerusalem.

Glory to the Father and to the Son and to the Holy Spirit, both now and ever and unto the ages of ages. Amen.

Alleluia, alleluia, alleluia. Glory to Thee, O God. *Thrice.*

Lord, have mercy. *Thrice.*

Troparia, Eighth Tone

Disregard my transgressions, O Lord Who wast born of a Virgin, and purify my heart, and make it a temple for Thy spotless Body and Blood. Let me not be rejected from Thy presence, O Thou Who hast great mercy without measure.

Glory to the Father and to the Son and to the Holy Spirit.
How can I who am unworthy dare to come to the Communion of Thy Holy Things? For if I should dare to approach Thee with those who are worthy, my garment betrayeth me, for it is not a festal robe, and I shall cause the condemnation of my greatly-sinful soul. Cleanse, O

Lord, the pollution from my soul, and save me, as Thou art the Lover of mankind.

Both now and ever and unto the ages of ages. Amen.

Greatly multiplied, O Theotokos, are my sins; unto Thee have I fled, O Pure One, imploring salvation. Do Thou visit mine enfeebled soul and pray to Thy Son and our God that He grant me forgiveness for the evil I have done, O Thou Only Blessed One.

During Holy and Great Lent say this:

When the glorious disciples were enlightened at the washing of the feet, then Judas the ungodly one was stricken and darkened with the love of silver. And unto the lawless judges did he deliver Thee, the Righteous Judge. Behold, O lover of money, him who for the sake thereof did hang himself; flee from that insatiable soul who dared such things against the Master. O Thou Who art good unto all, Lord, glory be to Thee.

Psalm 50

Have mercy upon me, O God, after Thy great goodness, and according to the multitude of Thy mercies do away mine offences. Wash me thoroughly from my wickedness, and cleanse me from my sin. For I know my fault, and my sin is ever before me. Against Thee only have I sinned, and done evil before Thee, that Thou mightest be justified in Thy words, and prevail when Thou art judged. For behold,

I was conceived in wickedness, and in sins did my mother bear me. For behold, Thou hast loved truth; the hidden and secret things of Thy wisdom hast Thou revealed unto me. Thou shalt sprinkle me with hyssop, and I shall be made clean; Thou shalt wash me, and I shall become whiter than snow. Thou shalt give joy and gladness to my hearing; the bones that have been humbled will rejoice. Turn Thy face from my sins, and put out all my misdeeds. Make me a clean heart, O God, and renew a right spirit within me. Cast me not away from Thy presence, and take not Thy Holy Spirit from me. O give me the comfort of Thy salvation, and stablish me with Thy governing Spirit. Then shall I teach Thy ways unto the wicked, and the ungodly shall be converted unto Thee. Deliver me from blood-guiltiness, O God, the God of my salvation, and my tongue shall rejoice in Thy righteousness. O Lord, open Thou my lips, and my mouth shall show forth Thy praise. For if Thou hadst desired sacrifice, I would have given it; but Thou delightest not in burnt offerings. The sacrifice unto God is a contrite spirit; a contrite and humble heart God shall not despise. O Lord, be favorable in Thy good will unto Zion, and let the walls of Jerusalem be builded up. Then shalt Thou be pleased with the sacrifice of righteousness, with oblation and whole-burnt offerings; then shall they offer young bullocks upon Thine altar.

And immediately, say this canon:

The Canon for Holy Communion

Second Tone

ODE 1

EIRMOS: Come, O ye people, let us sing a hymn to Christ our God, Who divided the sea and guided the people whom He brought out of the bondage of Egypt, for He is glorified.

REFRAIN: *Create in me a clean heart, O God, and renew a right spirit within me.*
May Thy holy Body be unto me the Bread of life eternal, O compassionate Lord, and Thy precious Blood be also the healing of many forms of illness.

REFRAIN: *Cast me not away from Thy presence, and take not Thy Holy Spirit from me.*
Defiled by unseemly deeds, I, the wretched one, am unworthy, O Christ, of the communion of Thy most pure Body and divine Blood, which do Thou vouchsafe me.

Glory to the Father and to the Son and to the Holy Spirit, both now and ever and unto the ages of ages. Amen.
O Blessed Bride of God, O good soil that grew the Corn untilled and saving to the world, vouchsafe me to be saved by eating it.

ODE 3

EIRMOS: By establishing me on the rock of faith, Thou

hast enlarged my mouth over mine enemies, for my spirit rejoiceth when I sing: There is none holy as our God, and none righteous beside Thee, O Lord.

Create in me a clean heart, O God, and renew a right spirit within me.

Teardrops grant me, O Christ, to cleanse my defiled heart, that, purified and with a good conscience, I may come with faith and fear, O Master, to the communion of Thy Divine Gifts.

Cast me not away from Thy presence, and take not Thy Holy Spirit from me.

May Thy most pure Body and divine Blood be unto me for remission of sins, for communion with the Holy Spirit and unto life eternal, O Lover of mankind, and to the estrangement of passions and sorrows.

Glory to the Father and to the Son and to the Holy Spirit, both now and ever and unto the ages of ages. Amen.

O Thou most holy table of the Bread of Life that for mercy's sake came down from on high, giving new life to the world, vouchsafe even me, the unworthy, to eat it with fear, and live.

ODE 4

EIRMOS: From a Virgin didst Thou come, not as an ambassador nor as an angel, but the very Lord Himself incarnate and didst save me, the whole man. Wherefore, I cry to Thee: Glory to Thy power, O Lord.

Create in me a clean heart, O God, and renew a right spirit within me.

O Thou Who wast incarnate for our sake, O Most-merciful One, Thou didst will to be slain as a sheep for the sin of mankind. Wherefore, I entreat Thee to blot out my sins also.

Cast me not away from Thy presence, and take not Thy Holy Spirit from me.

Heal the wounds of my soul, O Lord, and sanctify all of me, and vouchsafe, O Master, that I, the wretched one, may partake of Thy divine Mystical Supper.

Glory to the Father and to the Son and to the Holy Spirit, both now and ever and unto the ages of ages. Amen.

Propitiate for me also Him Who came from Thy womb, O Lady, and keep me, Thy servant, undefiled and blameless, so that by obtaining the spiritual Pearl I may be sanctified.

ODE 5

EIRMOS: O Lord, Giver of light and Creator of the ages, guide us in the light of Thy commandments, for we know none other God beside Thee.

Create in me a clean heart, O God, and renew a right spirit within me.

As Thou didst foretell, O Christ, so let it be unto Thy wicked servant, and in me abide, as Thou didst promise; for behold, I eat Thy divine Body and drink Thy Blood.

Cast me not away from Thy presence, and take not Thy Holy Spirit from me.

O Word of God and God, may the live coal of Thy Body be unto the enlightenment of me who am in darkness and Thy Blood unto the cleansing of my defiled soul.

Glory to the Father and to the Son and to the Holy Spirit, both now and ever and unto the ages of ages. Amen.

O Mary, Mother of God, precious tabernacle of fragrance, through Thy prayers make me a chosen vessel, that I may partake of the Sacrament of Thy Son.

ODE 6

EIRMOS: Whirled about in the abyss of sin, I appeal to the unfathomable abyss of Thy compassion: From corruption raise me up, O God.

Create in me a clean heart, O God, and renew a right spirit within me.

O Saviour, sanctify my mind, my soul, my heart and my body, and vouchsafe me uncondemned, O Master, to approach the fearful Mysteries.

Cast me not away from Thy presence, and take not Thy Holy Spirit from me.

Grant that I may be rid of passions and have the assistance of Thy grace and strengthening of life by the communion of Thy Holy Mysteries, O Christ.

Glory to the Father and to the Son and to the Holy Spirit, both now and ever and unto the ages of ages. Amen.

O Holy Word of God and God, sanctify all of me as I now come to Thy Divine Mysteries, through the prayers of Thy holy Mother.

Lord, have mercy. *Thrice.*

Glory to the Father and to the Son and to the Holy Spirit, both now and ever and unto the ages of ages. Amen.

Kontakion, Second Tone

Count me not unworthy, O Christ, to receive now the Bread which is Thy Body and Thy divine Blood and to partake, O Master, of Thy most pure and dread Mysteries, wretched though I be. Let these not be for me unto judgment, but unto life immortal and everlasting.

ODE 7

EIRMOS: The wise children did not serve the golden image, but went themselves into the flame and reviled the pagan gods. They cried in the midst of the flame, and the angel bedewed them: Already the prayer of your lips was heard.

Create in me a clean heart, O God, and renew a right spirit within me.

May the communion of Thine immortal Mysteries, the source of blessings, O Christ, be to me now light and life and dispassion and for progress and increase in the most divine virtues, O Only Good One, that I may glorify Thee.

Cast me not away from Thy presence, and take not Thy Holy Spirit from me.

That I may be delivered from passions and enemies, need and every sorrow, I now draw nigh with trembling, love and reverence, O Lover of mankind, to Thine immortal and divine Mysteries. Vouchsafe me to hymn Thee: Blessed art Thou, O Lord God of our fathers.

Glory to the Father and to the Son and to the Holy Spirit, both now and ever and unto the ages of ages. Amen.

O Thou Who art full of grace, Who beyond understanding gavest birth to Christ the Saviour, I Thy servant, the impure, now entreat Thee, the pure: Cleanse me, who am now about to approach the most pure Mysteries, from all defilement of flesh and spirit.

ODE 8

EIRMOS: God, Who descended into the fiery furnace

unto the Hebrew children and changed the flame into dew, praise Him as Lord, O ye works, and supremely exalt Him unto all ages.

Create in me a clean heart, O God, and renew a right spirit within me.

Of Thy heavenly and dread holy Mysteries, O Christ, and of Thy divine Mystical Supper vouchsafe now even me, the despairing one, to partake, O God my Saviour.

Cast me not away from Thy presence, and take not Thy Holy Spirit from me.

Fleeing for refuge to Thy loving-kindness, O Good One, with fear I cry unto Thee: Abide in me, O Saviour, and I, as Thou hast said, in Thee. For behold, presuming on Thy mercy, I eat Thy Body and drink Thy Blood.

Glory to the Father and to the Son and to the Holy Spirit, both now and ever and unto the ages of ages. Amen.

I tremble at taking fire, lest I be consumed as wax and grass. O fearful Mystery! O the loving-kindness of God! How is it that I, being but clay, partake of the divine Body and Blood, and am made incorruptible?

ODE 9

EIRMOS: The Son of the unoriginate Father, God and Lord, hath appeared unto us incarnate of the Virgin, to enlighten those in darkness and to gather the dispersed. Wherefore, the all-hymned Theotokos do we magnify.

Create in me a clean heart, O God, and renew a right spirit within me.

Christ It is, O taste and see! The Lord for our sake made like unto us of old, once offered Himself as an offering to His Father and is ever slain, sanctifying those who partake.

Cast me not away from Thy presence, and take not Thy Holy Spirit from me.

May I be sanctified in soul and body, O Master, may I be enlightened, may I be saved, may I become Thy dwelling through the communion of Thy holy Mysteries, having Thee with the Father and the Spirit living in me, O Benefactor plenteous in mercy.

Glory to the Father and to the Son and to the Holy Spirit.

May Thy Body and Thy most precious Blood, O my Saviour, be unto me as fire and light, consuming the substance of sin and burning the thorns of passions and enlightening all of me to worship Thy Divinity.

Both now and ever and unto the ages of ages. Amen.

God took flesh of Thy pure blood; wherefore, all generations do hymn Thee, O Lady, and throngs of heavenly minds glorify Thee, for through Thee they have clearly seen Him Who ruleth all things endued with human nature.

And immediately:

It is truly meet to bless Thee, the Theotokos, ever-blessed and most blameless and Mother of our God. More honorable than the Cherubim and beyond compare more glorious than the Seraphim, Who without corruption gavest birth to God the Word, the very Theotokos, Thee do we magnify.

Holy God, Holy Mighty, Holy Immortal, have mercy on us. *Thrice.*

Glory to the Father and to the Son and to the Holy Spirit, both now and ever and unto the ages of ages. Amen.

O Most Holy Trinity, have mercy on us. O Lord, blot out our sins. O Master, pardon our iniquities. O Holy One, visit and heal our infirmities for Thy name's sake.

Lord, have mercy. *Thrice.*

Glory to the Father and to the Son and to the Holy Spirit, both now and ever and unto the ages of ages. Amen.

Our Father, Who art in the heavens, hallowed be Thy name. Thy kingdom come, Thy will be done, on earth as it is in heaven. Give us this day our daily bread, and forgive us our debts, as we forgive our debtors; and lead us not into temptation, but deliver us from the evil one.

And the troparion of the day, if it be the feast of the Lord's Nativity, or another feast. If it be a Sunday, the Sunday troparion of the tone (see Appendix 1). If not, these:

SIXTH TONE: Have mercy on us, O Lord, have mercy on us; for at a loss for any defense, this prayer do we sinners offer unto Thee as Master: Have mercy on us.

Glory to the Father and to the Son and to the Holy Spirit.
Lord, have mercy on us, for we have hoped in Thee, be not angry with us greatly, neither remember our iniquities; but look upon us now as Thou art compassionate, and deliver us from our enemies; for Thou art our God, and we, Thy people; all are the works of Thy hands, and we call upon Thy name.

Both now and ever and unto the ages of ages. Amen.
THEOTOKION: The door of compassion open unto us, O blessed Theotokos, for hoping in Thee, let us not perish; through Thee may we be delivered from adversities, for Thou art the salvation of the Christian race.

Then:

Lord, have mercy. *Forty.*

And reverences [bows, prostrations], as many as thou desirest. And thereafter these lines:

If thou desirest, O man, to eat the Body of the Master,
Approach with fear, lest thou be burnt; for It is fire.
And when thou drinkest the Divine Blood unto communion,
First be reconciled to those who have grieved thee,
Then dare to eat the Mystical Food.

Other lines:

Before partaking of the awesome Sacrifice
Of the life-giving Body of the Master,
After this manner pray with trembling:

A Prayer of St. Basil the Great, 1

O Master Lord Jesus Christ our God, Source of life and immortality, Creator of all things visible and invisible, the co-eternal and co-unoriginate Son of the unoriginate Father, Who out of Thy great goodness didst in the latter days clothe Thyself in flesh and wast crucified and buried for us ungrateful and evil-disposed ones and hast renewed with Thine Own Blood our nature corrupted by sin: Do Thou Thyself, O Immortal King, accept the repentance of me, a sinner, and incline Thine ear to me, and hearken unto my words. For I have sinned against heaven and before Thee, and I am not worthy to look upon the height of Thy glory; for I have angered Thy goodness by transgressing Thy commandments and not obeying Thine injunctions. But Thou, O Lord, Who art not vengeful, but long-suffering and plenteous in mercy, hast not given me over to be destroyed with my sins, but always Thou awaitest my complete conversion. For Thou hast said, O Lover of mankind, through Thy prophet: For I desirest not the death of the sinner, but that he should return and live. For Thou desirest not, O Master, to destroy the work of Thy hands, neither shalt Thou be pleased with the destruction of men, but desirest that all be saved and come to a knowledge of the truth. Wherefore, even I, although unworthy of heaven and earth and of this temporal life, having submitted my whole self to sin and made myself a slave of pleasure, and having defaced Thine image, yet being Thy work and creation, wretched though I be, I despair not of my salvation and dare to approach Thine immeasurable loving-kindness. Accept then even me, O Lord, Lover of mankind, as Thou didst accept the sinful woman, the thief, the publican and the prodigal; and take away the heavy burden of my sins, Thou Who takest away the sin of the world and healest the infirmities of mankind; Who callest the weary and heavy-laden unto Thyself and givest them rest, Who camest not to call the righteous, but sinners to repentance. And do Thou cleanse me from all defilement of flesh and spirit and teach me to achieve holiness in fear of Thee; that with the pure testimony of my conscience, receiving a portion of Thy Holy Things, I may be united unto Thy holy Body and Blood and have Thee living and abiding in me with the Father and Thy Holy Spirit. Yea, O Lord Jesus Christ my God, let not the communion of Thine immaculate and life-giving Mysteries be unto me for judgment, neither unto infirmity of soul and body because of my partaking of them unworthily; but grant me until my last breath to receive without condemnation the portion of Thy Holy

Things, unto communion with the Holy Spirit, as a provision for life eternal, for an acceptable defense at Thy dread judgment seat; so that I also, with all Thine elect, may become a partaker of Thine incorruptible blessings, which Thou hast prepared for those who love Thee, O Lord, in whom Thou art glorified unto the ages. Amen.

A Prayer of Our Father among the Saints, John Chrysostom, 2

O Lord my God, I know that I am not worthy nor sufficient that Thou shouldest enter beneath the roof of the temple of my soul, for all is empty and fallen, and Thou hast not in me a place worthy to lay Thy head; but as from on high Thou didst humble Thyself for our sake, do Thou now also lower Thyself to my lowliness; and as Thou didst consent to lie in a cave and in a manger of dumb beasts, so consent also to lie in the manger of mine irrational soul and to enter into my defiled body. And as Thou didst not refuse to enter and to dine with sinners in the house of Simon the Leper, so deign also to enter into the house of my lowly soul, leprous and sinful. And as Thou didst not reject the harlot and sinner like me, when she came and touched Thee, so be compassionate also with me a sinner, as I approach and touch Thee. And as Thou didst feel no loathing for the defiled and unclean lips of her who kissed Thee, do Thou also not loathe my defiled lips nor mine abominable and impure mouth and my polluted and unclean tongue. But let the fiery coal of Thy most holy Body and Thy precious Blood be unto me for sanctification and enlightenment and health for my lowly soul and body, unto the lightening of the burden of my many sins, for preservation from every act of the devil, for the expulsion and prohibition of mine evil and wicked habits, unto the mortification of the passions, unto the keeping of Thy commandments, unto the application of Thy divine grace, unto the acquiring of Thy kingdom. For not with disdain do I approach Thee, O Christ God, but as one trusting in Thine ineffable goodness, and that I may not by much abstaining from Thy Communion become the prey of the spiritual wolf. Wherefore do I entreat Thee, for Thou art the only Holy One, O Master: Sanctify my soul and body, my mind and heart, my belly and inward parts, and renew me entirely. And implant Thy fear in my members, and make Thy sanctification inalienable from me, and be unto me a helper and defender, guiding my life in peace, vouchsafing me also to stand at Thy right hand with Thy saints, through the intercessions and supplications of Thy most pure Mother, of Thine immaterial ministers and immaculate hosts and of all the saints who from the ages have been pleasing unto Thee. Amen.

A Prayer of St. Symeon Metaphrastes, 3

O only pure and sinless Lord, Who through the ineffable compassion of Thy love for mankind didst take on all of our substance from the pure and virgin blood of Her Who bare Thee supernaturally through the descent of the Divine Spirit and the good will of the everlasting Father; O Christ Jesus, Wisdom of God and Peace and Power, Thou Who through the assumption of our nature didst take upon Thyself Thy life-giving and saving Passion—the cross, the nails, the spear and death: mortify the soul-corrupting passions of my body. Thou Who by Thy burial didst lead captive the kingdom of hades, bury with good thoughts mine evil schemes, and destroy the spirits of evil. Thou Who by Thy life-bearing resurrection on the third day didst raise up our fallen forefather, raise me up who have slipped down into sin, setting before me the ways of repentance. Thou Who by Thy most glorious Ascension didst deify the flesh that Thou hadst taken and didst honor it with a seat at the right hand of the Father, vouchsafe me through partaking of Thy holy Mysteries to obtain a place at Thy right hand among those who are saved. O Thou Who by the descent of Thy Spirit, the Comforter, didst make Thy holy disciples worthy vessels, show me also to be a receptacle of His coming. Thou Who art to come again to judge the world in righteousness, deign to let me also meet Thee on the clouds, my Judge and Creator, with all Thy saints; that I may endlessly glorify and praise Thee, with Thine Unoriginate Father and Thy Most-holy and good and life-creating Spirit, now and ever and unto the ages of ages. Amen.

Of the divine St. John Damascene, 4

O Master Lord Jesus Christ our God, Who alone hast authority to remit the sins of men: Do Thou, as the Good One and Lover of mankind, overlook all mine offences, whether committed with knowledge or in ignorance. And vouchsafe me to partake without condemnation of Thy Divine, glorious, immaculate and life-giving Mysteries; not as a burden, nor for punishment, nor for an increase of sins, but unto purification and sanctification and as a pledge of the life and kingdom to come, as a bulwark and help, and for the destruction of enemies and for the blotting out of my many transgressions. For Thou art a God of mercy and compassion and love for mankind, and unto Thee do we send up glory, with the Father and the Holy Spirit, now and ever and unto the ages of ages. Amen.

Of St. Basil the Great, 5

I know, O Lord, that I partake unworthily of Thine immaculate Body and Thy precious Blood and that I am guilty and that I eat and drink damnation to myself, not discerning the Body and Blood of Thee, my Christ and God; but taking courage from Thy compassion I approach Thee Who hast said: He who eateth My Flesh and drinketh My Blood abideth in Me and I in him. Show compassion, therefore, O Lord, and do not accuse me, a sinner, but deal with me according to Thy mercy; and let these Holy Things be for me unto healing and purification and enlightenment and preservation and salvation and unto sanctification of soul and body; unto the driving away of every fantasy and evil practice and activity of the devil working mentally in my members; unto confidence and love toward Thee, unto correction of life, unto steadfastness, unto an increase of virtue and perfection, unto fulfillment of the commandments, unto communion with the Holy Spirit, as a provision for life eternal, as an acceptable defense at Thy dread tribunal, not unto judgment or condemnation. Amen.

A Prayer of St. Symeon the New Theologian, 6

From sullied lips, from an abominable heart, from a tongue impure, from a soul defiled, accept my supplication, O my Christ, and disdain me not, neither my words, nor my ways, nor my shamelessness. Grant me to say boldly that which I desire, O my Christ. Or rather, teach me what I ought to do and say. I have sinned more than the sinful woman who, having learned where Thou wast lodging, bought myrrh and came daringly to anoint Thy feet, my God, my Master and my Christ. As Thou didst not reject her when she drew near from her heart, neither, O Word, be Thou filled with loathing for me, but grant me Thy feet to clasp and kiss and with floods of tears, as with most precious myrrh, may I dare to anoint them. Wash me with my tears, and purify me with them, O Word; remit also my transgressions, and grant me pardon. Thou knowest the multitude of mine evils, Thou knowest also my sores, and Thou seest my wounds; but also Thou knowest my faith, and Thou beholdest my good intentions, and Thou hearest my sighs. Nothing is hidden from Thee, my God, my Creator, My Redeemer, neither a teardrop, nor a part of a drop. My deeds not yet done Thine eyes have seen, and in Thy book even things not yet accomplished are written by Thee. See my lowliness, see my toil, how great it is, and all my sins take from me, O God of all; that with a pure heart, a trembling mind and a contrite soul I may partake of Thy spotless and most holy Mysteries, by which all who eat and drink in purity of heart are quickened and deified. For Thou, O my Master, hast said: Everyone who eateth My Flesh and drinketh My Blood abideth in Me and I in him. True is every word of my Master and God; for whosoever partaketh of the divine and deifying grace is no more alone, but with Thee, my Christ, the three-sunned Light Who enlighteneth the world. And that I may not remain alone without Thee, the Life-giver, my Breath, my Life, my Rejoicing, the Salvation of the world, therefore have I drawn nigh unto Thee, as Thou seest, with tears and with a contrite soul. O Ransom of mine offences, I ask Thee to receive me and that I may partake without condemnation of Thy life-giving and perfect Mysteries, that Thou mayest remain, as Thou hast said, with me, a thrice-wretched one, lest the deceiver, finding me without Thy grace, craftily seize me and having beguiled me, draw me away from Thy deifying words. Wherefore, I fall down before Thee and fervently cry unto Thee: As Thou didst receive the prodigal and the sinful woman who drew near, so receive me, the prodigal and profligate, O Compassionate One. With contrite soul I now come to Thee. I know, O Saviour, that none other hath sinned against Thee as have I, nor hath wrought the deeds that I have done. But this again I know, that neither the magnitude of mine offences nor the multitude of my sins surpasseth the abundant long-suffering of my God and His exceeding love for mankind; but with sympathetic mercy Thou dost purify and illumine those who fervently repent and makest them partakers of the light, sharers of Thy divinity without stint. And, strange to angels and to the minds of men, Thou conversest with them oftimes, as with Thy true friends. These things make me bold, these things give me wings, O Christ. And taking courage from the wealth of Thy benefactions to us, rejoicing and trembling at once, I partake of Fire, I that am grass. And, strange wonder! I am bedewed without being consumed, as the bush of old burned without being consumed. Now with thankful mind and grateful heart, with thankfulness in my members, my soul and body, I worship and magnify and glorify Thee, my God, for blessed art Thou, both now and unto the ages of ages. Amen.

Another Prayer of St. John Chrysostom, 7

O God, loose, remit and pardon me my transgressions wherein I have sinned against Thee, whether by word, deed or thought, voluntarily or involuntarily, consciously or unconsciously; forgive me all, for Thou art good and the Lover of mankind. And through the intercessions of Thy most pure Mother, Thy noetic ministers and holy hosts, and all the saints who from the ages have been pleasing unto Thee, deign to allow me without condemnation Thy holy and immaculate Body and precious Blood, unto the healing of soul and body and unto the purification of mine evil thoughts. For Thine is the kingdom and the power and the glory, with the Father and the Holy Spirit, now and ever and unto the ages of ages. Amen.

Of the same, 8

I am not sufficient, O Master and Lord, that Thou shouldst enter under the roof of my soul; but as Thou dost will as the Lover of mankind to dwell in me, I dare to approach Thee. Thou commandest: I shall open the doors which Thou alone didst create, that Thou mayest enter with Thy love for mankind, as is Thy nature, that Thou mayest enter and enlighten my darkened thought. I believe that Thou wilt do this, for Thou didst not drive away the sinful woman when she came unto Thee with tears, neither didst Thou reject the publican who repented, nor didst Thou spurn the thief who acknowledged Thy kingdom, nor didst Thou leave the repentant persecutor to himself; but all of those who came unto Thee in repentance Thou didst number among Thy friends, O Thou Who alone art blessed, always, now and unto endless ages. Amen.

Of the same, 9

O Lord Jesus Christ my God, loose, remit, cleanse and forgive me, Thy sinful and unprofitable and unworthy servant, my transgressions and offences and fallings into sin, which I have committed against Thee from my youth until the present day and hour, whether consciously or unconsciously, whether by words or deeds or in thought or imagination, in habit and in all my senses. And through the intercessions of Her Who seedlessly gave Thee birth, the Most Pure and Ever-Virgin Mary, Thy Mother, the only hope that maketh not ashamed and my mediation and salvation, vouchsafe me without condemnation to partake of Thine immaculate, immortal, life-giving and awesome Mysteries, unto the remission of sins and for life eternal, unto sanctification and enlightenment, strength, healing and health of both soul and body and unto the consumption and complete destruction of mine evil reasonings and intentions and prejudices and nocturnal fantasies of dark and evil spirits; for Thine is the kingdom and the power and the glory and the honor and the worship, with the Father and Thy Holy Spirit, now and ever and unto the ages of ages. Amen.

Another Prayer, of St. John Damascene, 10

I stand before the doors of Thy temple, yet I do not put away evil thoughts. But do Thou, O Christ God, Who didst justify the publican and didst have mercy on the woman of Canaan and didst open the doors of paradise to the thief, open unto me the abyss of Thy love for mankind, and receive me as I come and touch Thee, as Thou didst receive the woman with an issue of blood and the sinful woman. For the one received healing easily by touching the hem of Thy garment, while the other, by clasping Thy most pure feet, carried away absolution of sins. And I, a wretch, daring to receive Thy whole Body, let me not be consumed by fire; but receive me, as Thou didst receive them, and enlighten my spiritual senses, burning up my sinful errors; through the intercessions of Her Who seedlessly gave Thee birth and of the Heavenly Hosts, for blessed art Thou unto the ages of ages. Amen.

Another Prayer of St. John Chrysostom

I believe, O Lord, and I confess that Thou art truly the Christ, the Son of the living God, Who came into the world to save sinners, of whom I am chief. Moreover, I believe that this is truly Thy most pure Body, and this is truly Thine Own precious Blood. Wherefore, I pray Thee: Have mercy on me and forgive me my transgressions, voluntary and involuntary, whether in word or deed, in knowledge or in ignorance. And vouchsafe me to partake without condemnation of Thy most pure Mysteries, unto the remission of sins and life everlasting. Amen.

When coming to partake, say to thyself these lines of St. Symeon Metaphrastes:

Behold, I approach the Divine Communion.
O Creator, let me not be burnt by communicating,
For Thou art Fire, consuming the unworthy.
But, rather, purify me of all impurity.

Then again say:

Of Thy Mystical Supper, O Son of God, receive me today as a communicant; for I will not speak of the Mystery to Thine enemies; nor will I give Thee a kiss, as did Judas, but like the thief do I confess Thee: Remember me, O Lord, in Thy kingdom.

Furthermore, these lines:

Be awe-stricken, O mortal, beholding the deifying Blood;
For It is a fire that consumeth the unworthy.
The Divine Body both deifieth and nourisheth me.
It deifieth the spirit and wondrously nourisheth the mind.

Then the Troparia:

Thou hast sweetened me with Thy love, O Christ, and by Thy Divine zeal hast Thou changed me. But do Thou consume my sins with immaterial fire, and vouchsafe me to be filled with delight in Thee; that, leaping for joy, O Good One, I may magnify Thy two comings.

Into the brilliant company of Thy saints how shall I, the unworthy, enter? For if I dare to enter into the bride-chamber, my garment betrayeth me, for it is not a wedding garment, and I shall be bound and cast out by the angels. Cleanse, O Lord, my soul of pollution, and save me, as Thou art the Lover of mankind.

Then the Prayer:

O Master, Lover of mankind, O Lord Jesus Christ my God, let not these Holy Things be unto me for judgment, through my being unworthy, but unto the purification and sanctification of soul and body, and as a pledge of the life and kingdom to come. For it is good for me to cleave unto God, to put my hope of salvation in the Lord.

And again:

Of Thy Mystical Supper, O Son of God, receive me today as a communicant; for I will not speak of the Mystery to Thine enemies; nor will I give Thee a kiss, as did Judas, but like the thief do I confess Thee: Remember me, O Lord, in Thy kingdom.

The Prayers after
Holy Communion

When thou hast received the good Communion of the life-giving Mystical Gifts, give praise immediately, give thanks greatly, and from the soul say fervently unto God these things.

Glory to Thee, O God.
Glory to Thee, O God.
Glory to Thee, O God.

Then this

Prayer of Thanksgiving

I thank Thee, O Lord my God, that Thou hast not rejected me, a sinner, but hast vouchsafed me to be a communicant of Thy Holy Things. I thank Thee that Thou hast vouchsafed me, the unworthy, to partake of Thy most pure and heavenly Gifts. But, O Master, Lover of mankind, Who for our sake didst die and didst rise again and didst bestow upon us these dread and life-giving Mysteries for the well-being and sanctification of our souls and bodies, grant that these may be even unto me for the healing of both soul and body, for the averting of everything

91

hostile, for the enlightenment of the eyes of my heart, for the peace of the powers of my soul, for faith unashamed, for love unfeigned, for the fullness of wisdom, for the keeping of Thy commandments, for an increase of Thy Divine grace and for the attainment of Thy kingdom; that being preserved by them in Thy holiness, I may always remember Thy grace and no longer live for myself, but for Thee, our Master and Benefactor; and thus when I shall have departed this life in hope of life eternal, I may attain unto everlasting rest, where the sound of those who keep festival is unceasing, and the delight is endless of those who behold the ineffable beauty of Thy countenance. For Thou art the true desire and the unutterable gladness of those who love Thee, O Christ our God, and all creation doth hymn Thee unto the ages of ages. Amen.

Of St. Basil the Great, 2

O Master Christ God, King of the ages, and Creator of all things, I thank Thee for all the good things which Thou hast bestowed upon me and for the Communion of Thy most pure and life-giving Mysteries. I pray Thee, therefore, O Good One and Lover of Mankind: Keep me under Thy protection and in the shadow of Thy wings and grant me, even until my last breath, to partake worthily, with a pure conscience, of Thy Holy Things, unto the remission of sins and life eternal. For Thou art the Bread of Life, the Source of holiness, the Giver of good things; and unto Thee do we send up glory, together with the Father and the Holy Spirit, now and ever and unto the ages of ages. Amen.

Verses of St. Symeon Metaphrastes, 3

O Thou who givest me willingly Thy Flesh as food, Thou Who art Fire that doth consume the unworthy, burn me not, O my Creator; but, rather, enter Thou into my members, into all my joints, my reins, my heart. Burn up the thorns of all my sins. Purify my soul, sanctify my thoughts. Strengthen my substance together with my bones. Enlighten my simple five senses. Nail down the whole of me with Thy fear. Ever protect, preserve and keep me from every soul-corrupting deed and word. Purify and cleanse and adorn me; make me comely, give me understanding and enlighten me. Show me to be the dwelling-place of Thy Spirit alone and no longer the habitation of sin; that from me as Thine abode through the entry of Communion, every evildoer, every passion, may flee as from fire. As intercessors I offer unto Thee all the saints, the commanders of the bodiless hosts, Thy Forerunner, the wise apostles, and further, Thine undefiled pure Mother, whose entreaties do Thou accept, O my compassionate Christ, and make Thy servant a child of light. For Thou alone art our sanctification, O Good One, and the radiance of our souls, and unto Thee as God and Master, we all send up glory, as is meet, every day.

Another Prayer

O Lord Jesus Christ our God, may Thy holy Body be unto me for life eternal, and Thy precious Blood for the remission of sins; and may this Eucharist be unto me for joy, health and gladness. And at Thy dread Second Coming vouchsafe me, a sinner, to stand at the right hand of Thy glory, through the intercessions of Thy most pure Mother and of all the saints.

To the Most Holy Theotokos

O Most Holy Lady Theotokos, light of my darkened soul, my hope, protection, refuge, consolation, my joy: I thank Thee that Thou hast vouchsafed me, who am unworthy, to be a partaker of the most pure Body and precious Blood of Thy Son. O Thou Who gavest birth to the True Light, do Thou enlighten the spiritual eyes of my heart; Thou Who gavest birth to the Source of immortality, revive me who am dead in sin; Thou Who art the lovingly-compassionate Mother of the merciful God, have mercy on me, and grant me compunction and contrition in my heart and humility in my thoughts and the recall of my thoughts from captivity. And vouchsafe me until my last breath to receive without condemnation the sanctification of the most pure Mysteries, for the healing of both soul and body; and grant me tears of repentance and confession, that I may hymn and glorify Thee all the days of my life, for blessed and most glorified art Thou unto the ages of ages. Amen.

Then:

Now lettest Thou Thy servant depart in peace, O Master, according to Thy word; for mine eyes have seen Thy salvation which Thou hast prepared before the face of all peoples, a light of revelation for the Gentiles and the glory of Thy people Israel.

Holy God, Holy Mighty, Holy Immortal, have mercy on us. *Thrice.*

Glory to the Father and to the Son and to the Holy Spirit, both now and ever and unto the ages of ages. Amen.

O Most Holy Trinity, have mercy on us. O Lord, blot out our sins. O Master, pardon our iniquities. O Holy One, visit and heal our infirmities for Thy name's sake.

Lord, have mercy. *Thrice.*

Glory to the Father and to the Son and to the Holy Spirit, both now and ever and unto the ages of ages. Amen.

Our Father, Who art in the heavens, hallowed be Thy name. Thy kingdom come, Thy will be done, on earth as it is in heaven. Give us this day our daily bread, and forgive us our debts, as we forgive our debtors; and lead us not into temptation, but deliver us from the evil one.

Troparion to St. John Chrysostom, Eighth Tone

Grace shining forth from thy mouth like a beacon hath illumined the universe and disclosed to the world treasures of uncovetousness and shown us the heights of humility; but while instructing by thy words, O Father John Chrysostom, intercede with the Word, Christ our God, to save our souls.

Glory to the Father and to the Son and to the Holy Spirit.

Kontakion, Sixth Tone

From the heavens hast thou received divine grace and by thy lips thou dost teach all to worship the One God in Trinity, O John Chrysostom, all-blessed righteous one. Rightly do we acclaim thee, for thou art a teacher revealing things divine.

Both now and ever and unto the ages of ages. Amen.
O protection of Christians that cannot be put to shame, O mediation unto the Creator unfailing, disdain not the suppliant voices of sinners; but be Thou quick, O Good One, to help us who in faith cry unto Thee; hasten to intercession and speed Thou to make supplication, Thou Who dost ever protect, O Theotokos, those who honor Thee.

But if it be the Liturgy of St. Basil the Great, read the:

Troparion to St. Basil, First Tone

Thy fame hath gone forth into all the earth, which hath received thy word. Thereby thou hast divinely taught the Faith; thou hast made manifest the nature of created things; thou hast made the moral life of men a royal priesthood. O Basil our righteous father, intercede with Christ God that our souls be saved.

Glory to the Father and to the Son and to the Holy Spirit.

Kontakion, Fourth Tone

Thou didst prove to be an unshakable foundation of the Church, giving to all mortals an inviolate lordship, and sealing it with thy doctrines, O righteous Basil, revealer of heavenly things.

Both now . . .
O protection of Christians *(see preceding page).*

But if it be the Liturgy of the Presanctified Gifts, read the:

Troparion to St. Gregory the Dialogist, Fourth Tone

Thou who hast received of God divine grace from on high, O glorious Gregory, and hast been fortified by His power, thou didst will to walk according to the Gospel; wherefore, thou hast received of Christ the reward of thy labors, O all-blessed one. Entreat Him that He save our souls.

Glory to the Father and to the Son and to the Holy Spirit.

Kontakion, Third Tone

Thou hast shown thyself to be a leader like unto the Chief Shepherd Christ, O Father Gregory, guiding flocks of monks into the heavenly sheepfold, and from whence thou didst teach the flock of Christ His commandments. And now thou dost rejoice with them and dance in the heavenly mansions.

Both now and ever and unto the ages of ages. Amen.

O protection of Christians that cannot be put to shame, O mediation unto the Creator unfailing, disdain not the suppliant voices of sinners; but be Thou quick, O Good One, to help us who in faith cry unto Thee; hasten to intercession and speed Thou to make supplication, Thou Who dost ever protect, O Theotokos, those who honor Thee.

Lord, have mercy. *Twelve.*

Glory to the Father and to the Son and to the Holy Spirit, both now and ever and unto the ages of ages. Amen.

More honorable than the Cherubim and beyond compare more glorious than the Seraphim, Who without corruption gavest birth to God the Word, the very Theotokos, Thee do we magnify.

And the Dismissal.

Sunday Troparia

First Tone

TROPARION: When the stone had been sealed by the Jews, and the soldiers were guarding Thine immaculate Body, Thou didst arise on the third day, O Saviour, granting life unto the world. Wherefore, the Hosts of the heavens cried out to Thee, O Life-giver: Glory to Thy resurrection, O Christ. Glory to Thy kingdom. Glory to Thy dispensation, O only Lover of mankind.

Second Tone

TROPARION: When Thou didst descend unto death, O Life Immortal, then didst Thou slay hades with the lightning of Thy Divinity. And when Thou didst also raise the dead out of the nethermost depths, all the hosts of the heavens cried out: O Life-giver, Christ our God, glory be to Thee.

Third Tone

TROPARION: Let the heavens be glad; let earthly things rejoice; for the Lord hath wrought might with His arm. He hath trampled down death by death; the firstborn of the dead hath He become. From the belly of hades hath He delivered us and hath granted to the world great mercy.

Fourth Tone

TROPARION: Having learned the joyful proclamation of the resurrection from the angel and having cast off the ancestral condemnation, the women disciples of the Lord spake to the apostles exultantly: Death is despoiled and Christ God is risen, granting to the world great mercy.

Fifth Tone

TROPARION: Let us, O faithful, praise and worship the Word, Who is co-unoriginate with the Father and the Spirit, and Who was born of the Virgin for our salvation; for He was pleased to ascend the cross in the flesh and to endure death and to raise the dead by His glorious resurrection.

Sixth Tone

TROPARION: Angelic hosts were above Thy tomb, and they that guarded Thee became as dead. And Mary stood by the grave seeking Thine immaculate Body. Thou didst despoil hades and wast not tempted by it. Thou didst meet the Virgin and didst grant us life. O Thou Who didst rise from the dead, O Lord, glory be to Thee.

Seventh Tone

TROPARION: Thou didst destroy death by Thy cross; Thou didst open paradise to the thief. Thou didst change the lamentation of the myrrh-bearers, and Thou didst command Thine apostles to proclaim that Thou didst arise, O Christ God, and grantest to the world great mercy.

Eighth Tone

TROPARION: From on high didst Thou descend, O Compassionate One; to burial of three days hast Thou submitted, that Thou mightest free us from our passions. O our Life and Resurrection, O Lord, glory be to Thee.

On the Participation of the Faithful in the Eucharist

The Eucharist is the main Sacrament of the Church, instituted by our Lord Jesus Christ on the eve of His saving Passion, death upon the Cross, and Resurrection. To participate in the Eucharist and to partake of the Body and Blood of Christ is commanded by our Saviour who through His disciples said to all Christians: "Take, eat; this is My Body." . . . "Drink of it, all of you. For this is My blood of the new covenant, which is shed for many for the remission of sins." (Matt 26:26–28). The Church herself is the Body of Christ and, therefore, the Sacrament of the Body and Blood of Christ visibly manifests the mystical nature of the Church, building up the ecclesial community.

The spiritual life of an Orthodox Christian is inconceivable without the communion of the Holy Mysteries. Receiving the Holy Gifts, the faithful are sanctified by the power of the Holy Spirit and are united with Christ our Saviour and with each other, making one Body of Christ.

The Sacrament of the Eucharist requires special preparation. In the Church, the time itself – be it the span of a human life or the entire history of mankind – is an expectation and preparation for the encounter with Christ, while the entire rhythm of liturgical life is an expectation and preparation for the Divine Liturgy and, accordingly, for communion, for which sake the Liturgy is celebrated [in the first place].

I.

The practice of communion and the preparation for communion has changed and taken different forms throughout the history of the Church.

Already in the apostolic period, the tradition was established in the Church to celebrate the Eucharist every Sunday (and, if possible, even more often, e.g. on the days of martyrs' commemorations), so that Christians might remain in unending communion with Christ and with each other (see, e.g. 1 Cor 10:16–17; Acts 2:46; Acts 20:7). All members of the local community took part in the weekly Eucharist and received communion, while the refusal to take part in the Eucharistic communion without solid grounds was subject to condemnation:

> All the faithful who come in and hear the Scriptures, but do not stay for the prayers and the Holy Communion are to be excommunicated, as causing disorder in the Church (Apostolic canon 9).

The early Christian practice of communion at every Divine Liturgy remains an ideal even for the present time, as part of the Tradition of the Church.

At the same time, the growth in membership of the Church in the third and especially the fourth centuries led to some changes that altered liturgical life. As the number of the martyrs' commemorations and feast days increased, Eucharistic liturgies began to be celebrated more frequently – however, the presence at these assemblies for every Christian was considered to be merely desirable, but not mandatory. The Church has countered this tendency with the following canonical regulation:

> All who enter the church of God and hear the Holy Scriptures, but do not communicate with the people in prayers, or who turn away, by reason of some disorder, from the holy partaking of the Eucharist, are to be cast out of the Church, until, after they shall have made confession, and having brought forth the fruits of penance and made earnest entreaty, they shall have obtained forgiveness (canon 2, Council of Antioch).

Nevertheless, the sublime ideal of constant readiness for the reception of Holy Mysteries became hard to attain for many Christians. For this reason, already in the writings of the Holy Fathers of the fourth century we find evidence for the co-existence of different customs with regard to the regularity of communion. Thus, St. Basil the Great refers to communion four times a week as normative:

> And to receive communion every day and to partake of the holy Body and Blood of Christ is good and beneficial, for [Christ] himself clearly says: 'He who eats my flesh and drinks my blood, has

eternal life.' ... We receive communion four times every week: on Sunday, on Wednesday, on Friday, and on Saturday, and on other days, if there happens to be a memorial of a Saint (Letter 93 [89]).

But less than half a century later, St. John Chrysostom remarks that some, including monastics, started receiving communion only once or twice a year:

Many partake of this sacrifice once in the whole year, others twice; others many times. Our word then is to all; not to those only who are here, but to those also who are settled in the desert. For they partake once in the year, and often indeed at intervals of two years. What then? Which shall we approve? Those [who receive] once [in the year]? Those who [receive] many times? Those who [receive] few times? Neither those [who receive] once, nor those [who receive] often, nor those [who receive] seldom, but those [who come] with a pure conscience, from a pure heart, with an irreproachable life. Let such draw near continually; but those who are not such, not even once (Homilies on the Hebrews 17.7).

In the fourth century, the rule concerning the mandatory Eucharistic fast, which emerged already in the pre-Nicene period, was definitively established, mandating a complete abstinence from food and drink on the day of communion until the reception of Christ's Holy Mysteries: "May the holy sacrament of the altar be celebrated by the people who have not eaten" (canon 41/50 of the Council of Carthage, reaffirmed by canon 29 of the Council in Trullo). However, already in the late fourth – the beginning of the fifth century some Christians started to associate communion not only with the observance of Eucharistic abstinence before the Liturgy, but with the time of Great Lent in general, as attested by St John Chrysostom. The saintly bishop himself, however, was urging his flock for a more frequent communion:

Tell me, I beseech you, when after a year you partake of Communion, do you think that the Forty Days are sufficient for you for the purifying of the sins of all that time? And again, when a week has passed, do you give yourself up to the former things?

Tell me now, if when you have been well for forty days after a long illness, you should again give yourself up to the food which caused the sickness, have you not lost your former labor too? For if natural things are changed, much more those which depend on choice. . . . You assign forty days for the health of the soul, or perhaps not even forty, and do you expect to propitiate God? . . . These things I say, not as forbidding you to approach once a year, but as wishing you to draw near continually (Homilies on Hebrews 17.7).

By the eleventh and twelfth centuries in Byzantium, among monastics, the tradition was established to receive communion only when it was preceded by a discipline of preparation that included fasting, the examination of one's conscience before the spiritual father of the monastery, and the reading before communion of a special prayer rule which emerged and began to develop in that period. Pious laypeople began to take their direction from this same tradition, because monastic spirituality in Orthodoxy was always perceived as an ideal. In its strictest form this tradition is represented, e.g., in the directives of the Russian Typicon (chapter 32) which, in contrast with the Greek Typicon, mentions a mandatory seven-days fast before communion.

In 1699 an article titled "Instructional Notice" (Uchitel'noe izvestie) was included as an appendix to the Russian Sluzhebnik (Euchologion). This article contains, among other things, a directive concerning a mandatory term of preparation for holy communion: whoever desires, may partake during the four long fasting periods, while outside of these fasts, one must fast for seven days – this period, however, can be reduced:

If they desire to approach the holy communion outside of the four usual fasts, let them fast for seven days beforehand, remaining constant in prayers at church and at home – this is for those who are not in need, when in need, let them fast only for three days or for one day.

In practice, an extremely stringent approach toward preparation for holy communion, which had its positive spiritual aspects, led also to the fact that some Christians were abstaining from communion for a long time, citing their need for worthy preparation. The norm, con-

tained in the Spiritual Regulation (1721), mandating that all Christians
in the Russian Empire must receive communion at least once a year,
was precisely directed against this practice of rare communion:

> Every Christian must receive the Holy Eucharist frequently,
> but at least once a year. For this is our most eloquent thanksgiv-
> ing to God for such salvation accomplished for us by the death
> of the Saviour ... For this reason, if any Christian is shown to
> abstain long from Holy Communion, by this he shows himself
> to be not in the Body of Christ, that is, he is not a communicant
> of the Church.

In the nineteenth and early twentieth centuries pious people sought
to receive communion at least during every one of the lengthy fasting periods. Many saints of that time, among them St. Theophan
the Recluse and Righteous John of Kronstadt, called the people to
approach the Holy Mysteries even more frequently. As St Theophan
said, "a measure [to commune] once or twice a month – is the most
measured," even though "one can say nothing disapproving" regarding a more frequent communion. Every faithful may be guided by
these words of this Saint:

> Try to receive communion of the Holy Mysteries more fre-
> quently, as your spiritual father will permit. But try always to
> approach with due preparation and, moreover, with fear and
> trembling, lest, by getting accustomed, you start approaching
> with indifference.

The struggle of the Church during the years of persecution in the
twentieth century motivated many clergymen and laity to reject the
practice of infrequent communion that existed previously. In par-
ticular, on May 13, 1931 the Provisional Patriarchal Synod stated in its
resolution:

> [Be it resolved that] the desire that an Orthodox Christian
> receives communion as often as possible, and those more
> advanced among them – even every Sunday, may be deemed
> acceptable.

At the present time, many Orthodox Christians receive communion much more frequently than the majority of Christians in pre-revolutionary Russia. However, the practice of frequent communion cannot be automatically expanded unto all the faithful without exception, for the frequency of communion is directly dependent upon a person's spiritual and moral state, so that the faithful, to use Chrysostom's words, may approach the communion of the Holy Mysteries "with a pure conscience, as much as it is possible for us."

II.

The requirements for preparation before Holy Communion are determined for each member of the faithful by the definitions and regulations of the Church, which are applied by each spiritual father, taking into consideration the frequency with which the person receives the Holy Mysteries, his spiritual, moral, and physical state, the external circumstances of his life, such as his occupation or whether he is overburdened by taking care for those close to him.

A person's spiritual father is a priest to whom a Christian regularly confesses, who is familiar with the circumstances of his life and his spiritual state. The faithful may go to confession to other priests if it is impossible for them to confess to their own spiritual father. If a faithful Christian does not have a spiritual father, he should address the questions relating to the reception of communion to the priests of the church where he desires to receive.

Both the spiritual father – who is guided by ecclesiastical definitions and regulations and, based on them, gives direction to a Christian as well as the communicant, need to understand that the goal of preparation does not lie in an external fulfillment of formal prerequisites, but in the acquisition of a penitent state of soul, the forgiveness of offenses, reconciliation with one's neighbors, and, finally, attaining union with Christ in the Holy Mysteries. Fasting and prayer are means to assist the person preparing for communion to acquire this inner state.

Remembering the words of our Saviour, who denounced those who impose upon the people heavy burdens hard to bear (see Matt 23:4), spiritual fathers need to understand that unjustified strictness, as well as excessive leniency, can impede a person's union with our Saviour Christ and can harm him spiritually. The preparation of monastics for their participation in the Sacrament of the Eucharist is performed in accordance with the Statute on Monasteries and Monasticism, as well as following the statutes of specific monasteries.

1.

The practice of fasting in preparation for communion is regulated by the ascetic tradition of the Church. The fasting as abstinence from animal products and abstaining from distractions, accompanied by assiduous prayer and repentance traditionally precedes the communion of the Holy Mysteries. The length and extent of fasting before Holy Communion can differ, depending on the Christian's inner state and objective life circumstances. Particularly, in the case of an acute or chronic illness that requires special dietary rules, as well as during pregnancy and nursing a child for women, the time of fasting can be shortened, lightened, or set aside altogether. The same rule concerns Christians who temporarily or permanently live in secular institutions which presuppose living and taking meals in common (military units, hospitals, boarding schools, special schools, or prisons).

The practice that has taken shape in our time that every one who receives communion several times a year fasts for three days before communion fully corresponds to the tradition of the Church. At the same time, the practice when a person who receives communion on a weekly basis or several times a month, while observing lengthy and one-day fasts established by the Typicon, approaches the holy Chalice without any additional fasting or keeping a fast on the day or in the evening before communion, is acceptable as well. This matter has to be resolved with the blessing of the person's spiritual father. The requirements concerning preparation for holy communion, intended for the laypeople who receive communion frequently, are also applicable for members of the clergy.

Bright Week, the week following the feast of Christ's Pascha, creates a special case regarding the practice of preparation for Holy Communion. The ancient canonical norm regarding the obligatory participation of all faithful at the Sunday Eucharist was in the seventh century expanded to include all of the Divine Liturgies during Bright Week:

From the holy day of the Resurrection of Christ our God until the New Sunday, for a whole week, in the holy churches the faithful ought to be free from labor, rejoicing in Christ with psalms and hymns and spiritual songs; and celebrating the feast, and applying their minds to the reading of the Holy Scriptures, and delighting in the Holy Mysteries; for thus shall we be exalted with Christ and together with him be raised up (canon 66 of the Council in Trullo).

It follows from this canon that the laypeople are called to receive communion during the liturgies of Bright Week. Considering that the Typicon does not foresee any fasting during Bright Week and that Bright Week is preceded by seven weeks of struggle in the course of Lent and Holy Week, it ought to be acknowledged that the practice that has been established in many parishes of the Russian Orthodox Church that Christians who observed the Great Fast receive Holy Communion during Bright Week, while limiting their fasting to abstaining from food after midnight, is fully consistent with the canonical tradition of the Church. Similar practice can be expanded to the period between Nativity and Theophany. Those who prepare for communion during these days should take special care from excessive consumption of food and drink.

2.

One should distinguish the preparatory fast from the Eucharistic fast in a proper sense, i.e. the complete abstinence from food and drink from midnight until Holy Communion . This fast is mandated by the canons (see canon 41/50 of Carthage, cited above). At the same time, the requirement of Eucharistic fast is not applied to infants, as well as to persons who suffer from grave acute or chronic illnesses which demand a regular intake of medicine or food (e.g. diabetes), and to those who are dying. Moreover, at the discretion of the spiritual father, this requirement may be facilitated for women who are pregnant or nursing a child.

Canon law prescribes abstinence from marital relations during the period of preparation for Holy Communion . Canon 5 of Timothy of Alexandria refers to such abstinence on the eve of communion.

The Church encourages those Christians who suffer from the harmful habit of smoking tobacco to abandon this habit. Those, however, who do not yet have the strength to do so must abstain from smoking from midnight and, if possible, from the evening before communion.

Since in accordance with the Typicon, the Liturgy of the Presanctified Gifts is combined with Vespers, its celebration during the evening hours constitutes a liturgical norm (even though in practice this liturgy usually is celebrated in the morning). In accordance with the decision of the Holy Synod of the Russian Orthodox Church of November 28, 1968:

> When the Divine Liturgy of the Presanctified Gifts is celebrated in the evening, the abstention from food and drink for those who receive communion must be no less than six hours. However the abstention before communion from midnight of the day is quite praiseworthy and those who have physical strength may keep it.

One should also apply the standard of no less than six hours of abstinence while preparing for communion at the Divine Liturgy that is celebrated during the night (e.g. on the feasts of Holy Pascha and the Nativity of Christ).

3.

The preparation for communion consists not only in abstinence from certain food, but also includes the more regular attendance of church services, and in the performance of a rule of prayer.

The Order of preparation for Holy Communion, consisting of a special canon and prayers, is an inalienable part of this prayerful preparation. The prayer rule usually also includes the canons to the Saviour, the Theotokos, the Guardian Angel and other prayers (see "The Rule for those who are preparing to serve and wish to partake of the Holy Divine Mysteries of the Body and Blood of our Lord Jesus Christ" in the Liturgical Psalter [Sledovannaya Psaltir']). During Bright Week, the prayer rule consists of the Paschal canon, and also the canon and prayers before communion. A personal rule of prayer should be recited outside of services, which always presuppose the joint prayer of the entire assembly. Special pastoral care should be given to the people whose spiritual path in the Church is just beginning, and who are not yet accustomed to lengthy prayer rules, as well as to children and those who are ill. The Liturgical Psalter presupposes a possibility to replace canons and akathists with the Jesus prayer and prostrations. In the spirit of this direction, with a blessing of the spiritual father, the above-mentioned rule of prayer may be substituted by other prayers.

Since the Liturgy is the summit of the whole liturgical cycle, the attendance at the services that precede the Liturgy – primarily, Vespers and Matins (or the Vigil) – is an important part of preparation for the partaking of the Holy Body and Blood of Christ.

If a person was absent at the evening services on the eve of communion or did not recite his prayer rule in its fullness, his spiritual father or a priest who hears his confession must urge him to a more thorough preparation for communion, but also must take into account the circumstances of his life and possible existence of excusable reasons.

Preparing themselves for the reception of the Holy Mysteries of Christ at the Divine Liturgy, the children of the Church must gather in the temple before the service begins. To come late for the Divine Liturgy, especially when the faithful arrive after the reading of the Epistle and the Gospel demonstrates neglect toward the Mystery of the Body and Blood of Christ. If such tardiness occurs, the priest who hears confessions or distributes communion may decide not to admit such a person to the Holy Chalice. Exception can be made for people with limited physical capabilities, nursing mothers, small children, and the adults who accompany them.

After the end of the Divine Liturgy, a Christian must hear in church or himself read the thanksgiving prayers after Holy Communion. While prayerfully giving thanks to God for the gift he has received, a Christian must strive by all means to preserve this gift in peace, piety, and love for God and neighbor.

Considering the unbreakable bond between communion and the Divine Liturgy, the clergy must not permit the practice where in some churches the faithful are prohibited from receiving Holy Communion on the feasts of Holy Pascha, the Nativity of Christ, Theophany, on Memorial Saturdays, and on the Day of Rejoicing (Radonitsa).

III.

A person who is preparing for Holy Communion performs an examination of his conscience, which presupposes a sincere repentance for the sins he has committed and revealing of these sins before the priest in the Sacrament of Repentance. In the situation where many who come to our churches are not yet fully rooted in the church life, and consequently sometimes do not understand the meaning of the Sacrament of the Eucharist or are not aware of the moral and canonical consequences of their sinful deeds, confession allows the priest who hears confession to discern whether it is possible to allow the penitent to receive the Holy Mysteries of Christ.

In special cases, in accordance with the practice that has formed in many parishes, a spiritual father may allow a layperson to partake of the Body and Blood of Christ several times during the same week (e.g. during Holy or Bright Week) without coming to confession before every communion, excluding the situations when a person desiring to receive communion perceives a need for confession. While giving this blessing to the faithful, spiritual fathers should particularly remember their great responsibility for the souls of their flock, which was placed upon them in the sacrament of ordination.

In some parishes, it takes a long time to wait for the communion of the laity to begin. This occurs due to the length of communion of the clergy during liturgies with many concelebrants or due to the hearing of confessions after the communion verse. This state of affairs should be seen as undesirable. The sacrament of repentance must be, if possible, performed outside of Divine Liturgy, lest the penitent and the confessing priest both be deprived from full participation in the joint Eucharistic prayer. It is unacceptable for a priest assisting at the liturgy to hear confessions during the reading of the Gospel or during the Eucharistic canon. It is desirable to hear confessions in the evening before the Divine Liturgy or before the beginning of the liturgy. Moreover, it is important to establish in parishes the fixed days and hours when a priest would always be present [in church] to meet those who desire to talk with their pastor.

IV.

It is unacceptable to receive communion in a state of resentment or anger, or with grave, unconfessed sins or unforgiven offenses. Those who dare to approach the Eucharistic gifts in such a state of soul place themselves under divine judgment, in accordance with the words of the Apostle: "For he who eats and drinks in an unworthy manner eats and drinks judgment to himself, not discerning the Lord's body. For this reason many are weak and sick among you, and many sleep." (1 Cor 11:29–30).

When grave sins have been committed, the application of the canons regarding excommunication of a person for an extended period of time (for longer than one year) may be performed only with the blessing of the diocesan bishop. When a priest abuses his right to impose penances, his case may be brought for review by the ecclesiastical court.

The canons prohibit receiving communion during one's menses (canon 2 of St. Dionysius of Alexandria, canon 7 of Timothy of Alexandria). An exception may be made in case of a danger of death, and whenever the issue of blood continues for a long time due to chronic or acute illness.

V.

As it was stated in the Bases for Social Concept of the Russian Orthodox Church (10.2) and in the definition of the Holy Synod of the Russian Orthodox Church of December 28, 1998, the Church, while insisting upon the necessity for ecclesiastical marriage, still does not deprive from communion of the Holy Mysteries the spouses who constitute a marital union contracted with the acceptance of all legal rights and duties and recognized as a legally valid marriage, but which was not for some reasons sanctified by the rite of crowning. This measure of ecclesial economy is grounded in the words of St. Paul (1 Cor 7:14) and canon 72 of the Council in Trullo, and intends to make it more possible to live the life of the Church for those Orthodox Christians who entered their marriage before the beginning of their conscious participation in the Church's sacraments. In contrast with adulterous cohabitation, which is a canonical impediment for communion, the former union constitutes a legal marriage in the eyes of the Church (excepting the cases when legally permissible "marriages," e.g. between close relatives or same-sex cohabitations, recognized in a number of countries, are from the Church's point of view unacceptable in principle). The duty of pastors, however, is to remind the faithful of the necessity not only to contract a legally valid marriage, but also to sanctify such marriage through the liturgical rite of the Church.

Special attention is given to cases when persons have lived together for a long time, often having children together, but are not united either through ecclesiastical or a state-recognized marriage – moreover, one of the persons in this cohabitation does not desire either to register their relationship or to marry in Church. Such cohabitations are sinful and their wide dissemination in the world demonstrates the rebellion against the divine purpose concerning man, endangers the institution of marriage and cannot receive any recognition from the Church. At the same time, the spiritual father who knows the life situation of a specific person and condescends to human weakness, may in exceptional cases admit to communion the person in this relationship who is aware of the sinfulness of such cohabitation and seeks to enter a lawful marriage. The person in this cohabitation, guilty of preventing this marriage from taking place, cannot be admitted to communion. If, however, at least one of the cohabiting persons is married to another person, both sides cannot be admitted to communion without canonical rectification of their condition and offering an appropriate penance.

VI.

The preparation of children for Holy Communion has its own special characteristics. The length of this preparation is determined by the parents with the advice of their spiritual father and must take into consideration the child's age, state of health, and the extent of his integration into the life of the Church.

Parents who regularly bring their children to the Holy Chalice, which is a good thing, must seek to receive communion together with them (if it is not possible for both parents to receive, then one parent at a time). The practice where parents bring children to communion, but themselves seldom receive communion, prevents the development in a child's mind of a sense of need to partake of the Eucharistic meal.

The first confession before communion, in accordance with canon 18 of Timothy of Alexandria, is performed after the child has reached ten years of age, but in the tradition of the Russian Orthodox Church the first confession usually occurs at seven years of age. At the same time, the age of the first confession, as well as the frequency of confession for a child between seven and ten years of age, if he receives communion every Sunday, must be determined by the spiritual father and the parents together, considering the individual characteristics in the child's development and his understanding of the life of the Church.

The Eucharistic fast is not mandatory for children until three years of age. According to tradition, beginning with the age of three years, Orthodox families gradually teach the child to abstain from food and drink before communion of the Holy Mysteries. By the age of seven years, a child must be firmly accustomed to receive on an empty stomach. From this time, the child should be instructed to read the prayers before Holy Communion , the content and length of which is determined by the parents in accordance with the child's age, as well as his spiritual and intellectual development.

The sponsors of the child must fully participate in rearing the children in piety, which includes urging the children toward regular partaking of the Holy Mysteries of Christ and helping the parents to bring the children to the Holy Chalice.

✠ ✠ ✠

The Eucharist is the central Sacrament of the Church. Regular communion is necessary for a human being for salvation, in accordance with the words of our Lord Jesus Christ:

> "Most assuredly, I say to you, unless you eat the flesh of the Son of Man and drink His blood, you have no life in you. Whoever eats My flesh and drinks My blood has eternal life, and I will raise him up at the last day. (John 6:53–54).

Translated from the Russian language.
Document of the Hierarchal Consultation of
the Russian Orthodox Church
February 2015, Cathedral of Christ the Saviour in Moscow